CISTERCIAN STUDIES SERIES: NUMBER ONE HUNDRED THIRTY-SIX

Matthew Kelty

THE CALL OF WILD GEESE

CISTERCIAN STUDIES SERIES: NUMBER ONE HUNDRED THIRTY-SIX

THE CALL OF WILD GEESE
More Sermons in a Monastery

by

MATTHEW KELTY

Edited, with an introduction, by

WILLIAM O. PAULSELL

Cistercian Publications
Kalamazoo, Michigan — Spencer, Massachusetts

© Copyright, Cistercian Publications, Inc., 1996
The work of Cistercian Publications is made possible in part
by support from Western Michigan University to
The Institute of Cistercian Studies

Available from

Cistercian Publications (Distribution)
St Joseph's Abbey
167 North Spencer Road
Spencer MA 01562-1233

Editorial Offices
Cistercian Publications
Institute of Cistercian Studies
Western Michigan University
Kalamazoo MI 49008

*To Marion
after all*

TABLE OF CONTENTS ❧

INTRODUCTION ❧

Matthew Kelty at eighty is as irrepressible as ever. Several years ago a volume of his homilies, *Sermons in a Monastery*,[1] appeared. Preached at the Abbey of Gethsemani in Kentucky in the 1960s, these homilies were remarkable for their strong imagery and provocative ideas.

Since that decade Matthew has moved to Oxford, North Carolina, to organize a small experimental community under the sponsorship of Gethsemani. After three years there he went to Papua New Guinea, where he had earlier been a missionary, to take up the hermit life. He lived in solitude for nine and a half years, producing an autobiographical book, *Flute Solo*[2] and many letters, some of which were collected in *Letters from a Hermit*.[3] Eventually Matthew returned to Gethsemani, enriched by the solitary experience, to resume a more traditional Cistercian life.

During a brief visit one afternoon I was approached by another monk who suggested that I edit a second volume of homilies. 'Matthew has done some fine work since he returned from New Guinea,' the monk said to me. 'You really ought to ask him for some more material.' When I approached him while on retreat a few months later, Matthew agreed. There soon appeared in my room a folder of photocopied manuscripts.

1. Cistercian Publications, 1983.
2. Andrews and McMeel, 1979.
3. Templegate, 1978.

All the homilies in this book were preached after his return from the hermitage. They reflect a more mature experience than the first volume. The imagery is still strong: geese flying in formation over the monastery, the darkness of the first Christmas, a bishop flying a Cessna, the depths of the human heart, an apparition of a dead monk, Jonah as Christ and as us. Those who know much about Gethsemani will appreciate several anecdotes about Father Louis, better known to the world as Thomas Merton.

In reading these sermons we learn of the human realities of the monastic life and the monk's need for grace and mercy. Although these homilies were preached to monks, they are applicable generally, to any congregation of Christians, for human problems are the same in both church and cloister.

The importance of balancing male and female elements within a person is a continuing theme in Matthew's preaching, and his criticisms of modern society and its destructive *macho* values reflect his concern for a lack of tenderness in human life. Some of his themes, such as the hatred of God, are a bit unexpected, but challenging. His understanding of the place of pain and suffering in Christian faith will help many to see the meaning in their experiences. Undergirding all of his homilies is a profound devotion to Christ.

Father Matthew writes in long sentences using a stream of consciousness style, a challenge to any editor. Yet the homilies have about them a spontaneity and a quality of excitement not often found in somber modern preaching.

His friendship and spiritual guidance for the past quarter century are gifts I treasure. I hope these pieces are as stimulating to you as they have been to me.

Special thanks to Barbara Hall, a student at Lexington Theological Seminary, who first entered Matthew's homilies into my computer so that the editing process could begin.

W.O.P.

1

THE CALL OF WILD GEESE ❧

A few afternoons ago I was out back, burning trash, when I heard the unmistakable call of geese from far away to the north. It took me a while to find them high in the sky against dark clouds—mysterious, impressive, flying in splendid formation in that sweep of wing which is so majestic, so deliberate, a flock headed south with purpose.

But then, when they were just over Gethsemani the V-shape fell apart for some reason, and where there had been order there was chaos and a mess. Dissension. I thought, some want to stay over here like they did last year, some want to keep on going, or maybe it was just that the leader tired and no fresh goose was forthcoming. So they wheeled about, several hundred of them, with great noise, each telling others that something had to be done. Now and then a single goose would take a try at leadership and wing off with a few others following him, but no more would take it. It took ten or fifteen minutes for them to reach a consensus, and then, suddenly, one gander took the lead, the others followed, and in a matter of moments a great echelon appeared in the sky, the honking happiness resumed, and they were off to Nashville and the Gulf and Mexico beyond. And I went to Vespers thinking about it.

The readings in the Liturgy of the Hours and in the Eucharist these past several weeks have been pretty heavy, grim stuff, most of it, about the end of all things at the end of time, wild imagery and fiery horsemen carrying out the orders of an angry God. One brother asked me, 'Why do they read such stuff? The visitors must be very upset to hear all that.' 'Well,' I said, 'they are perhaps not the only ones to be upset. maybe it's something we ought to hear and think about.' Which says it, I think; for however you may describe it, and it is a challenge to the imagination, the end is to come one day, soon or late. The lesson is that this place, this earth, this universe, is temporal. It is not forever. Tennyson's brook that goes on forever, the eternal mountains and the everlasting seas, are poetry, not reality. It is all going one day. That much is certain. How, we are not so sure. When, certainly not. And what will follow is a rather vague scenario: something new, renewed, that we know. And, most strange of all, we are part of it. What makes such readings rather hard listening, it seems to me, is that we live in an age in which the end if very possible. If we cannot destroy the entire universe, we are capable of bringing an end to the planet that is home to us. The scriptures do not sound nearly as wild as they once did. An angry God is a possibility, our God.

If there is to be a final disintegration, we deal also with the collapse of a culture we live in. When whole cultural patterns fall part, we have a preview of the final act, and it is no less trying to the human soul than the actual performance. I do not spell out the details of this scene. Things do change. And they change enormously and they change fast. We live in the midst of disintegration. New things come, are in process, yet have not come yet. No consensus.

There is the personal apocalypse which is death. If the days of the world and the universe we know are numbered, if cultures shift and fade, so are our days, too. Come early, come late, the end will come, and the stars will fall from our heaven and the earth shake beneath our feet, the angels of God will come to announce the end of all things for us. Death, the great mystery is closer that today's sunset, for any one of us could be gone before the sun goes down this afternoon.

When the delightful order of the flying geese fell apart and confusion and chaos took over, I saw a fitting revelation of our feelings about the ultimate destiny of the world. How like the cultural confusion we know when patterns of behavior break down, values disappear, codes and cults collapse, everything gets loose and wild and crazy. Like the music that tells it, the world rocks and reels. Which again is the way we feel, I suspect, when death comes down our corridor, to our door, opens and enters. Everything we knew and loved slips away and we approach the edge of the cliff and know we are going over it in some mad dream.

The geese stayed together. None took off on their own. So, no panic. They knew there was a leader among them and they knew that whoever it was would emerge and be a leader all would accept, not one imposed. Nor could the honor be snatched by one to whom it was not given. When the leader emerged, something electric happened: they all agreed, they all followed, order returned, the journey began again. The happy honking told of their peace. When the leader emerged there was communion. Without communion you can never get anywhere. The geese would still be wheeling around Gethsemani skies if they did not know this. No community gets anywhere without leadership and without followship which is consensus in action. Fellowship without followship is fraternity-house theology, not Christianity. And followship without leadership is a kindergarten, for there is no communion of action. If the birds are not flying full with all they have, the pattern falls apart. There is no beauty without dedication to the common, to the love of Jesus with one another and for a dying world that so needs the witness of people who believe what they say. Who can make a pattern against the dark skies of our times? It can be a marvel of beauty to restore hope to the wondering and confused. We know where we're going and we know how to get there, and honey, we are on our way.

Faith, then, in the face of ultimate apocalypse, faith in the midst of mixed times, faith in the face of our own disintegration, is what we need. There is no magic, secret formula. We must affirm that God is in us and in our midst. Who guides geese guides us. We believe that. We mean it.

2

Come Away by Yourselves to a Lonely Place and Rest ❧

Some years ago, when one of the monks of the community began to articulate the hermit life in word and deed, a cartoon appeared in a popular magazine, perhaps with reference to that well-known monk. The drawing featured a bearded hermit before his cave and on either side a number of signboards with bold lettering announced, 'Fresh Baked Hermits A Dollar a Dozen'. Another said, 'Tours of the Hermitage Every Afternoon at Three'. Said a third, 'Cassettes Available on Aspects of the Hermit Life'. Another advertised, 'New Paperback: The World I Loved and Left, My Life as a Hermit'. The amusing thing about this, of course, was how close to truth was the wit.

There is one thing certain. If you go off by yourself as a person or as a community you can count on it: a path will be beaten to your door by people coming to see what you are up to. As in the Gospel, as here, and like Jesus, you will receive who comes. Saint Benedict says in his rule that guests are never wanting in a monastery. So, on the one hand you have people who see themselves solitary yet Christian, and therefore bound to give love and hospitality for the very people they seek to escape. Monks and monasteries catch themselves in this strange bind of being warm and friendly while acting cool and remote.

Our own house is still rather out of the way, even if not as remote today as it once was. But, say this much for us, we have yet to put up a sign telling the traveler this is it, or even how to get here. What sign is there out front is an historic marker put up by the state. As for that trifle at the end of Highway 247 in Culvertown, the county made that investment.

We keep changing the looks of the place. The fourteen chimneys that once gave the front wing some character went long ago, as did the shutters, changing the texture of the house. The massive steeple that had been a landmark for a century went twenty years ago. The quaint gate house that has been the front since who knows when is gone. And if that will not fool them, we are going to stucco the whole place white if we can find the money. The result: no one will recognize the monastery. In the face of that, an invisible front door does not seem especially formidable, nor does a front door that is narrow and leads to steep stairs and a gallery from which we are viewed from a safe distance. Real intimate.

What is the point of this stand-off? Indeed, what is the point, when you come to realize, as people do, that the monks are warm and friendly, hospitable people-lovers. Like the bean in biology class, we are dicotyledonous, two-sided. So there are mysteries here. For one thing, why do monks do the solitude thing? And for another, why is there such interest in what they do, for if it is odd to go off by oneself, it is just as odd to follow someone doing that. The one happens, so does the other.

One thing ought to be clear from the outset. This has nothing to do with a lack of feeling for women. Women have been excluded from monasteries and from much traffic with monks since the monastic movement began. Then you could get away with it because there was a lot of such segregation in civil society, like the men's bar in the Biltmore in New York where Dan Walsh first talked to Thomas Merton about Gethsemani. That society changes is society's privilege and monks can go along with such changes because they are part of society. That does not mean that they are suddenly not misogynists. They never were that, any more than cloistered nuns are man haters because men have not been and still are not permitted in their enclosures. But, when we kept women out that was at least half of humankind, and monks have wanted to keep all humankind at a distance. The game was already half won.

It is a matter of cutting down the input, of controlling what you are subjected to, of creating a context. We desire minimal input, a quiet context, a controlled environment. That is the idea. Cut out the outer to increase the inner. More quiet than most want, less input than many can abide. More control of the environment that many opt for. Why? Because by nature, by temperament, by character, by grace, we feel called to this. Maybe we are introverts.

Perhaps we are more heart than head, more cooperative than competitive, maybe more feminine than most men or more male than most women, more integrated. Not all of us are poets or dreamers or prophets or priests or writers or dramatists or artists or dancers, but many of us are the kind of persons who could be, might be, sometimes are. That sort. Without quiet such people perish. They go mad. They wilt. They languish and die.

It is hard to have quiet in the midst of bustle and noise, even good bustle and beautiful noise. Beethoven is noise when you get too much of him—not to mention rock. When you are in touch with your heart, when you live with your soul, when you know your own depths, you become in the process more wholly human, more nearly real, with it. When that happens, even to a modest degree, something splendid takes place. Everything changes around you. The world is a different world. You do not know what it is, but you do know that it cannot be doubted. It does not have much to do with virtue, though virtue helps. It is not intelligence, or prowess in technique, though they help too.

It is more a matter of allowing oneself to be human. When that happens, signals go out. Influence is created. Aura is born. Spirit becomes manifest. You cannot possibly hide it or explain it, but you will radiate it. The place will revel in it. And people will come from miles around, not knowing what they are really looking for, but certain when they get there that they have found it. They think it is the monks and give no one any peace until they have met one, only to discover it is not the monks after all. They are just like everyone else. What then? I know not. God knows. Whatever it is, it is released from the depths of the human when humans are willing to let it be released.

The joy of the monk is no less than the joy of those who share what he has, for the monk knows that it is a gift and gifts do not last unless shared. The monk is no capitalist who stakes out a claim in order to sell at a profit. No, he freely spends all he has as prodigally as the God who gave it all to him. The people he flees from are the people he carries in his heart, sings for, prays for, lives for, loves, and is glad to meet.

Knowing all the while that the spring will go dry, the fire will flicker out, the vine will wither, he is beholden to grace. Without it, the world shrivels, becomes a waste, old, bitter, angry, violent and doomed. So people come like sheep without a shepherd, a flock searching for green grass, for bread in the wilderness. Jesus feeds them, then off with them all, and he goes into the night and the hills alone to pray.

So they come to the monk, look him in the eyes and speak to him of God and ask, 'Is God?'

The monk replies, 'God is'.

And of God's love, 'Is it?'

And the monk replies, 'It is'.

'Me?'

'You.'

'Are you sure?'

'Yes, I am sure.'

'How sure are you?'

'So sure I lay my life on it.'

And the heart breaks in the person who cannot be contained for joy, for tears. What was known all along is known now. What was believed all along is believed now. What was too good to be true is true.

3

Every Reason to Be Merry ♣

Some fifty years ago, when the Depression was making its first inroads on life in this country, we had a President who achieved a reputation by having nothing to say. 'Silent Cal', more properly Calvin Coolidge, was thought, indeed, to have the wisdom of the ages. However, it takes more than a closed mouth to make a wise man. Calvin made this obvious with the observation, 'When more and more people are thrown out of work, unemployment results'. Given such profundity, it is no wonder that Dorothy Parker, a tart wit of the era, asked, when told that Coolidge was dead, 'And how could they tell?' for he was a dour man with no sensitivity, warm as New England granite, a compassionate tombstone, thin lips clamped shut.

We are like him when we go round saying, maybe mindlessly, 'Merry Christmas! Merry Christmas one and all! Joy to you. And peace.' I mean, saying it to people out of work, just to mention one thing. When the head of the house has lost a job, 'Merry Christmas?' Or worse, maybe, is faced with the prospect of losing it.

The monk says, with the delicacy of Silent Cal, 'Of course we have no unemployment in the monastery! Plenty of work!' And in any case, we monks do not think in terms of money, do we? Save for these last, cold months of the year, most of us have no part in income-producing labor. Only a few do. The rest of us serve in the kitchen, in the laundry, in the infirmary, in the library, in the sacristy, in the bindery, in the garage. No money in any of that, and probably not much in the farm either. In any case, it's just part of the larger scene, an aspect of our life as monks.

A monk walking through the woods came upon a couple strolling and answered their greetings. 'And what do you do?' the woman asked. The monk replied, 'I don't do anything. I live here.' She insisted. So did he. She thought of life in terms of what one does for a living, but the monk did not. He insisted that he did nothing, he only lived here. She was vexed.

It is not like this in the world around us, where one is known for what one does. People were once named for their work: smith, carter, wheelright, wainright, fletcher, thatcher, weaver, dyer, carpenter, shepherd, miller, clark, cooper. But, our identity as monks is with Christ, not with what we do.

Well said.

But are we perhaps as callous as Coolidge if we think this true only of monks? Is a person only a machine to make money? Is being a parent, a spouse, summed up in what a person does for a living? Is it how much you bring home that makes you what you are? If it is, many a wife and mother has little value, for in terms of economics she may be more like us monks, performing useful and necessary tasks and services. But there is no money in any of it.

No, my brothers. The monk is like any Christian, and any Christian is like a monk. And the likeness is in Christ. Making money is not the heart of Christ's life, nor ours, nor any Christian's life. Man or woman.

Which is why we can say Merry Christmas and mean it. For granted that having no income, no job, is a most dreadful worry, it is not the end of everything. Not the loss of humanity, identity, personhood. For trial, trouble, sickness and affliction and death are with us today as they were yesterday and will be tomorrow. Characteristic of life anywhere. Any time. Only in some times more than in others.

And so we can still say Merry Christmas with meaning. Still wish each other joy. Still exchange a kiss of peace. Nor does God begrudge us what happiness we may manage. And we share as we can with those who have less than we do. Yet we know too that we cannot solve all the world's problems, heal all the world's ills, fill the world's empty stomach, clothe the naked of the world. We do what we can. Monks too know pain and sorrow, sickness and death, even the loss of a job. I do not know as we should make too much of that, nor should we feel guilt over any joy God gives. No need to be grim Christians, wanting in the warmth that should be the first fruit of our contact with Christ.

We have every reason to be merry, and that, no matter what the scene may be, is our situation. For there is a God who is very good, who loves us very much. And with God's grace we hope to manage somehow, no matter what comes our way, for we are far more than what we have. It is what we are that is everything. We are children of God. Christmas proves it. Merry Christmas, everyone!

4

BORN IN THE NIGHT ❧

J esus was born in the night, in the dark. That is why we
have Mass at night. In the middle of the night Jesus Son
of God was born of the Virgin Mary. When the angel
Gabriel came to her and asked her if she were willing to
become the mother of Christ our redeemer, she said she was
not married, so how could this be? The angel said that Jesus
would not be born of man but of the Holy Spirit. The Holy
Spirit would come upon her and so she would conceive and
bear a child who would be named the Son of God.

Nine months later, when her time was near, the government
decreed a census and everyone had to go to his or her own
village. Since Joseph and Mary were of the house of David,
they both went to their own place, Bethlehem, in order to give
their names to the government. Because there were so many
people in their place, there was no house where they could find
a room, so they went outside the town to the hills where there
were caves in which people and cattle would stay. It was in such
a cave on the hillside that Jesus was born. After he was born
Mary let him go to sleep in a manger where they put food to
feed the cattle.

Out in those same hills were shepherds who were watching
their sheep so that dogs and wolves would not attack them.
They were on the hills in the middle of the night under the stars
when the whole of the heavens was filled with angels singing
a joyous song: 'Glory to God in the highest, peace on earth'.
The shepherds were frightened, but the angel told them not to
be afraid, but to go to one of the caves on the hillside where

they would find with his mother a newborn child who would be the Savior of the world. So the shepherds went and found the child and his mother and they told Mary about the angels of heaven and the good news they had brought, that here was the Savior of the world. The shepherds knelt and adored the child and then left and told everyone they could about what they had heard and seen.

Jesus was born in the night. Everything God does has a reason, so there is a reason also for this.

Most people everywhere are afraid of the dark. Darkness is a time when people do evil, for no one can see them. Thieves steal at night when all are asleep so they cannot be seen. People commit murder at night. They do other kinds of wrong. In many places people are afraid to go out at night, for night is a bad time.

The first thing people want in darkness is light. In ages past people who were up at night would sit around a fire so they could have light and see. If they had to walk about, they took fire with them. Fire was the only light people had for many centuries. Only after a long time did they learn that oil would burn and make a fire, oil from olives and oil from palm trees. They discovered that beeswax with a wick would burn so they made candles. Much later they learned that fish oil would burn. Later on they found oil in the ground made kerosene for lamps. It was only a few years ago that electricity was discovered and electric light brightened the gloom.

People have always tried to overcome darkness with light. Everyone wants light at night. People fear the dark for they associate darkness with evil. Christ, therefore, was born in the night, in the dark, because he came to conquer darkness and evil. He said, 'I am the light of the world'. He is the light of the world because by his passion and death he broke the power that evil has over people.

The night is still dark and there is still evil about, but just as we conquer darkness by light, so by Christ we can conquer evil.

For this little child who is born in darkness will one day die on the cross for us.

We must remember that evil and darkness are not outside us, in the night or in other people. Darkness and evil are inside each person. When we conquer this darkness and evil by the light of Christ, the light will overcome us. We do evil because we listen to the powers of darkness and evil inside us. These powers are very strong and we are not able to overcome them except with the help of God.

Jesus came to give us this help and we can have it if we want it. We ask for it when we pray. Prayer is talking with God, and when we speak to God we ask for help to avoid evil and do good, that this light may be always with us and we be not overcome with darkness.

Even today some people are very much afraid of darkness, of evil spirits, of bad dreams. We should not be afraid. God will always help us if we ask. God will not abandon us; we can always call upon Jesus. We make the sign of the cross on which Jesus died and call upon his holy name.

If you are afraid of the night, call upon Jesus and make the sign of the cross. If you are tempted to do wrong, call on Jesus and make the sign of the cross. When you leave your house, when you go to your garden, make the sign of the cross. When you go to bed at night, when you get up in the morning, make the sign of the cross and call upon Jesus. When you get on a plane, make the sign of the cross. When you begin to eat, when you begin to work, make the sign of the cross. This way we call on him to be our light in darkness, our strength against evil. This way we will have the peace the angels sang about the first Christmas night and will have the joy that God promised to all who would receive the light, cast off the works of darkness, and walk in his love.

5

CHRIST AND THE FAMILY ❧

When you speak to monks of the feast of the Holy Family you wonder what you ought most to call on: simplicity or courage, imagination or a highly developed moral sense, or just a willingness to talk about something not too appropriate.

The alternate prayer at the beginning of this Mass of the Holy Family mentions our need to grasp the holiness of human love. Yet the love we have in mind when we think of the family is perhaps not the kind that Jesus knew in the Holy Family. I would hazard that a wider sense of family than is common among us was his experience. Grandparents, uncles and aunts and cousins in great numbers would more likely have been his environment than merely Joseph and Mary and he, the only child. Primitive cultures see family life in broad relationships and in it a child grows up with a wide exposure to love and interest from many men and women and children.

It is easier to see the relation between our sort of monastic community and such a family. Even so, we are aware that calling a religious community a family is applicable only in a limited way. So many levels are not there that one is best counseled not to expect familial love in a cloister.

The sort of love that is here is not a lesser sort, but it is a different sort. Jesus came from a family, and yet never established one of his own; we ought not to neglect this aspect of his life. For one thing, it was unusual, and his own virginal life, not to say his birth from a virgin, was so striking in the background from which he came that the matter could in no sense have been incidental or of no great consequence. That is why the witness of the virginal life in the Church has been constant, and here we might draw a lesson from our pondering on these mysteries.

Joseph is not the model for the father of the family, Mary is not the model for the mother, and Jesus is not the model for the child. Jesus is the model for all. Christ is our Savior, our God. Grace comes from him. He teaches us and leads us. We follow him. The saints, including Mary and Joseph, inspire us because they lead us to Jesus.

One would tell a father, then: be like Christ. And one would tell a mother: be like Christ. Women are not Marians but Christians, and men are not Josephites but Christians. Christ is the model for all.

Because Christ was born of woman he was truly human, but he had no wife. This has worried some people and erring minds have even assumed that he was married, tradition notwithstanding; that he had brothers and sisters, not mere cousins, so he must have had a typical family life. The Church teaches that Christ was a virgin, of a virgin. He is a model for the human family because he was perfectly human, perfectly integrated, the summation of beauty and balance, human in the fullest, finest, most classic sense. He was not merely male. That is a term for a diminished man.

Think well on it. Both men and women are called upon to be like Jesus. This is a call to true wholeness.

Our society cruelly divides heaven and earth, man and woman, male and female. Christ unites them—in his own virginal life, first of all, then as model for married love, too. That is why one can speak to monks about the Holy Family, about human life and human love.

Christ as virgin had no family of his own. Can one say, therefore, that he had no love in his life? One cannot say that.

When we reduce Christ to male as we tend to reduce all men to males, not to say women to females, we run contrary to the

Gospel. In a word, Christ was both masculine and feminine because he was a complete human being, perfect.

At first blush we are prone to think such talk bizarre because our norms are taken from the world and not the Gospel. Violent, angry, aggressive, dominating, overlording males are not more human than Jesus, who was none of these. Gentle, tolerant, kind, pacific men are not more female than male. They are more truly human, though, and more nearly Christ-like.

Sexual identity makes one male or female, but not man or woman, a human person. There is a lot more to it than that, and Jesus is the model for that lot more.

Monasteries like this one, and the monks in them, have this among other purposes: to restate the norms by which the Christian lives, that is to say, to place Christ before us all as the one we follow and imitate in our growth towards wholeness.

The world is full of males passing as men and females passing as women. Christ calls us beyond pose to full love, in and out of marriage. This is why a monastery can be a house of happiness, wholeness, genuine love. Granted, it can be difficult to achieve all this when we come from a society whose values are not Christian. What worse blight for a monastery than men unwilling to be whole, afraid to be feminine, unable to be Christ-like?

The model is Christ and one has but to listen to the Gospel, enter into prayer, be nourished at the altar and dedicated to the life of love in order to come to wholeness and happiness. Christ is the head of the Holy Family and model for everyone in the human family.

May he lead us all to that wholeness and holiness and happiness we were born for, so that we might attain to the kingdom where they do not marry but are as the angels, whole, complete, integral through Christ our Lord.

6

Just Like His Father ♣

O nce in a while a brother who has had visitors in the guest house on the hill will tell you about the family of another brother who happened to be there at the same time. 'You know,' he says, with an element of surprise in his voice, 'you know, Brother so-and-so is just like his father, or just like his mother. Just like him.' The wonder, of course, is his surprise. But the surprise is not in the obvious family resemblance but in finding how true the obvious is. When you know a monk well, over many years, you more and more come to think of him as in some sense an original, a new creation. You know of course that all he has is derived, a given, but that does not temper your view if you have never met the source. One day you do and you see your living original is nothing of the sort. He is a reasonable facsimile of those who begot him. The throw of his head, the quality of his voice, his laugh, his gestures, his walk, yes even his looks are someone else's. Or a modified version, an interesting take-off. But derived. We all know that this is not always the case, but even then one learns to be cautious. If we saw a certain uncle or aunt, one or another of his grandparents, we might be surprised.

All of which leads to mercy. For if the brother inherits visible qualities and good ones, it is likely that frailties and oddities and strange quirks may be derived, too. Faults of character are often inherited, and it strikes you that the monk was given this collection of possibilities to see what he could make of it. Sometimes a lifetime is spent coping with it all, not to say what has been inflicted on him by unwitting or knowing abuse. So mercy rises in your heart toward him.

Mercy must rise in my heart and yours toward those who gave us life and everything that made up our beginnings. No family save one is all blessed. All are blemished, some more, some less. You and I and all of us fear the results. Mercy is the only answer to all that. Forgive. This means we must accept the truth and deny no reality. You cannot forgive what you are not willing to see, what you cannot bring yourself to acknowledge.

This is what family is all about: that mutuality that ties me to all who went before me, all who are my forebears, that uncounted number who are in some way unknown to me and yet very much a part of me. In our humanity we are tied in the most profound way to multitudes of people. I am a Celt and the syndrome that constitutes a Celt constitutes me, wholly individual, wholly original, totally derived, the human family.

It surely cannot do to think of the Holy Family as a model for us in the usual sense. A virginal mother, a virginal father, a divine child hardly constitute a norm that any family could align itself with. And even if the patriarchal family of Jesus' people has changed a great deal, families are still somewhat patriarchal. Anyone who has been out of Nelson County, Kentucky, or North America knows that the variety of human families is wide indeed. The American family is not typical, if there really is a typical American family. And even so, the family in the widest sense or the most specific is not a Christian invention nor is Christ's teaching on the family something that could not apply anywhere in the world, any time.

In much of the world today, the family is thought to be under attack, or changing, or disintegrating; your view perhaps reveals your base. Many developments are not acceptable to Christians who are Catholic. Apparently, cultures, like people, are at times subject to influences of destruction and can choose to drift into habits, modes, ways that lead to disaster. People can do this in a few years. Cultures take longer. Do we have a tendency to destroy and then rebuild? We live in a destructive time, a difficult time for families. There is not a great deal of support for traditional ways. And good people are often willing to abandon the traditional for something novel that looks as good if not better. One hopes they are not deceived.

The Church, it seems to me, is courageous in standing by the fundamentals and tries earnestly to be compassionate and merciful. It is not easy, dear friends, for Church or family. Counsel your brothers and your sisters, your nephews and your nieces, to go no further, and see for yourself how many are at odds with much that we take for granted.

So mercy is called for, but so is hope. The end of the world is not coming because patterns shift and ways change. The perduring values will emerge and grow strong again because the creative urge in the human is too great, too powerful. But it will still take much pain and suffering. Tearing down is easy, rebuilding is not. This is no time to condemn and find fault or wring our hands because things are not what they were or what we think they should be.

There are good people everywhere doing the best they can. They deserve our mercy and the inspiration of our hope. All you have and all I have came from others before me, before you, who loved as they could and did as they could mange. We look with mercy on all from whom we come and with mercy on all with whom we live this day and age on earth, our contemporaries now and for all eternity, this great family in which Christ has immersed himself and given a divine dimension it never had before. The divine that was in the Holy Family is the divine that is in ours. And this is true now and at any time, true anywhere in the world. The wild confusion of our own times will not make us blind to that. We are not strangers to chaos as we partake of the Holy Body and the Holy Blood every day. We know the divine family very well and we know the human family too. One hand in the one, one hand in the other, and we will not let either go.

There is something divine in every human being and in every human family. Christ came to release that divine and he does it by mercy. Be a monk of mercy if you would be a monk at all. Let no one say of us, 'They have it good, these monks do. They build themselves a heavenly city on earth, look forward with confidence to an eternal one and have not much use for the likes of us who have a poor city here below and not much hope for a better one to come.' No, sweet brother. You and I have within not only what father and mother gave, but through them a communion with all humankind. And in Christ we are one with all in a communion of God-kind. We are family, only family. Even so? Even so.

7

THE FEAST OF MARY ♣

The altar in this abbey church rests, as I suppose you are aware, on a vast concrete block which in turn rests on the ground. In other words, the connection between the earth and the altar is direct. In a sense that is quite correct, the altar rests on the earth. This is significant and deliberate. Not only is the altar certainly heavy; it is also firmly rooted in the earth. In primitive cultures in many parts of the world it was, even if it is not still so, customary to choose the bare earth for birth and death. Mothers liked to give birth close to the ground, close to the original matter. People liked to die close to the primal *mater*, the original matter, the source. In monastic lore it is not rare to hear of monks choosing to be placed on the ground or at least on the floor to die, perhaps scattered with ashes and earth. The same instinct. Altars of sacrifice, the major events of birth and death, are seen as vitally connected to the earth from which we come, the earth to which we shall all return, the cosmic womb from which we shall all one day emerge in the great rebirth, the awakening at the end of time.

We celebrate today the feast of Mary, Mother of God, the one who in some very particular way speaks of the earth, is our mother, our earthly mother. It is from her that Christ was born, he the Son of God. This earthly mother, then, is also the divine mother who gave birth to him who is literally the Son of God. It is not far-fetched to speak of earth as mother and heaven as father, to find it easy to relate to Mary as our Mother, to God as our Father, and to Jesus Christ as both Son of God and Son of Mary. It is through Mary that we take part in this drama of the marriage of heaven and earth.

Would you agree that it is important to see our life as monks as essentially involved in this basic business, this wondering on the mystery of heaven and earth, father and mother, god-kind and human-kind? I do not mean in terms of doctrine, things to study and be well informed on. This is indeed necessary, but it is not nearly enough. Learning is not wisdom, nor is knowledge holiness. It is one thing to study a mystery, another to ponder it. We here are called to ponder.

If we see ourselves called to a life of pondering, it is to see ourselves involved with elemental dialogue between God and humanity, earth and heaven, time and eternity, man and woman, matter and spirit, body and soul. These dualities are forever in relation and the establishment of a good relation is an arduous, a consuming work. This marriage of parties so disparate, so distant, and yet so drawn to one another that we are literally racked by their pulling. How general it is, indeed how simple, to let one dominate the other! And in this way to ease tension, to put to sleep troublesome dynamics.

A monastery is an effort to set up such an environment, such a live-in, so that this marriage not only can take place, but can develop with a happy speed and without the effort of which the average person is not capable. It aims to be a way of life in which the dualities of our human nature are respected and reverenced. Garnering the wisdom of past ages we follow a pattern of living which keeps body in living dialogue with soul without the one overwhelming the other. It is to know a way of working that does not make work the end–all and be–all—let alone the gathering of beautiful things or the accumulation of money or the pursuit of pleasure or power or other lusts and cravings to which we are all prone. Neither is it a surrender to mediocrity and life without challenge or ideal.

The Mother of God is a model in all this. We can scarcely think of ourselves as imitating her, for she was not trammelled by sin as we are. Yet we can try to be like her in the love of pondering the mysteries of which life is so full. For this we do not need great intelligence or much knowledge or profound skills—though these are blessed goods—but we do need the sort of introvert-light that our culture tries so hard to extinguish: we need some ability to enter into quiet and to live without feeing that excitement is necessarily a witness to real living. There is no need to know everything, to do everything, to see everything, to hear everything, to know everyone, to go everywhere. In fact, there is much truth in realizing that knowing less and doing less, and seeing less and hearing less, and so less all the way down the line, is perhaps the beginning of real wisdom.

Which of course is not it at all. For we are led to think that we need but follow that one law of less: less of everything, then we arrive. Be taboo the effort to reduce this way to rules and regulations, to absolute traditions and hallowed positions that are clung to in pertinacity, fought for, argued about, and championed in a way that ruins them and robs them of the good they might do. Children of darkness we can be.

It is not by running from one side of the ship to the other in times of trouble, but by rejecting panic and opting for willingness to hear both sides—since God gave us two ears—content to live with ambiguity, seeing it not as failure but as willingness to know the wholeness of things.

How hard our faith does drive us! What enormous leaps we are called to make. How gross our faith, for example, in its earthiness. For what belief is there that celebrates conception and birth and suffering and death as ours does? Fancy making a feast over the very act that we surround with secrecy, the Immaculate Conception of this holy woman who is our mother and the Lord's. Once in human history, thanks to God our Lord, something wholly and utterly beautiful was done and done without flaw or blemish, with no taint or suggestion of aboriginal evil. Once it was possible for a man and a woman to posit an act of love and have no regret. How lovely, how supremely, supremely lovely. How utterly earthly, too. And yet this sweet woman is to conceive in her womb a wonderful man not just by virtue of another of her kind, but by the Spirit of God, and he who is born is the Son of God. How unutterable. How beyond us! It is only because we are familiar with the story that we are not shocked by it. In this womb heaven and earth embrace and are united. This is not something answered by dogma. It is not enough to repeat the doctrine and accept it, as one might accept a scientific formula worked out by brilliant minds, and sound off $E=mc^2$ as if we knew what we were talking about. Jesus Christ is Son of God and Son of Mary. Easily said. Well said. But it will mean nothing at all, be only a formula, if we do not ponder it. And that is what we are here for, to ponder a lifetime on mystery.

Hence the walls. Hence the quiet, the chant and the monotony, the feast and the cold, the cowls and the cloister, the abbot and the two handled cups, the dark night, the hills and the familiar faces and wonted ways of the brethren. Slowly, slowly, as an old man's chin year by year sinks deeper into his chest, the mind, the heart, the powers of our being go low in the depths of the soul to read there the deep things of God in a language without words, impossible to speak of, not to say think about. Can a blind man tell you what he sees, a deaf person the sound of the music he hears, or the one in love explain it? The fruit of our pondering is as mute as the altar of sacrifice rooted in the earth and united to heaven.

8

CHRIST THE KING ♣

In 1925 Pius XI instituted the Feast of Christ the King. Much of the music composed for the Mass and Office seems to me to have been quite good, but good, bad, or indifferent, it is all gone. The feast remains, however, and in much religious thinking of the past decades, it seems now even more fitting than was perhaps first recognized. For, if Christ has always been King and if the Gospels declare as much, the special celebration of his kingship has been reserved for these latter times.

One likes to think that the scarcity of kings nowadays made this development easier. As long as there were many living kings in office in the world we know, it was not always in good taste to connect the Lord and Savior with the breed. There are Henrys and Richards and Charleses and Louises whose company is no great honor. Similarly, it would be somewhat awkward to call Christ our President and associate him with Johnson, Nixon, Harding, Coolidge and other worthies.

Yet we must be careful. The Lord was almost at pains to mingle, not merely with the poor and lowly, but with sinners, even sinful rulers. It would be an error to assume, I think, that kingship must be bleached of all stain before it can be applied to Christ the Lord. Even the saintly kings—however few—were quite human. The best were blemished.

Kingship is a secular business. So is being human, being on earth. To speak of Christ's kingdom is not merely a declaration that his Kingdom is far and away superior to any earthly facsimile. It is better to say and to see that kingship as such, being king, has by its state become something not merely secular but also sacred. Kingship now has a dignity it never had before. But so has being human, being alive, being here.

There is no such thing as secular any more. Or, if you like, no such thing as sacred. Or, to save theology, may we not say that sacred and secular are now wed?

When God became human, God did not disappear, nor did humanity. But, something new is at hand, we have one who is at once both God and human.

This human person is God; this God is a human person. This king is divine. This president is immortal. This reign is everlasting. This term of office eternal. Everything is changed by this fact. People are no longer merely people. Earth is no longer merely earth. There is nothing only secular. Mere bread now becomes body, mere wine blood. And divine Body. Divine blood.

Just what is going to happen at the end of time we really do not know. We have, as I understand it, just a few hints. I do not think it can be said that this world will perish, but it will be changed. That seems basic. Glorified. Transfigured. Renewed. What will be revealed is the sacrality of the secular, the holiness of the profane, the glory of the common.

Bread and wine and human flesh, human life, and human loss, kings and crowns and royal robes, pain and suffering and death, are somehow, in some way, caught up in the divine. It is for us, too, to be caught up in the divine, to enter it, be transfigured by it, that humankind become Godkind.

I thought of this the other week when we anointed the sick. We had Mass right afterwards, you recall. And that is what came to me: This is my body. This is my blood. Each of us can say: this is my body. And when disease and death come, this is my body you are breaking, this is my blood you are drinking. My life you are taking. Who is breaking? Who is drinking? The Lord of life and of death? Is God eating humanity? Or humanity consuming God? Whose life is this? Whose death? We are transformed into God. So we enter God's kingdom.

What we celebrate today has not happened yet. It is to come. But it happens every day, it comes every day, that ever-deepening mingling of God and humanity, heaven and earth, time and eternity.

It is not just that Grant Park became a church when John Paul said Mass there for a million, as the papers said. Or Phoenix Park. Or Yankee Stadium. Or the Mall in Washington. The world became a church when Jesus appeared in it, and everyone on earth is in that church. And in that church glorious praise is sung to the King of Kings and Lord of Lords. He who reigns forever and ever. Good music. Blessed are you if you can hear that music. More blessed if you can sing it. Amen.

9

TRINITY ♣

In the religious myths of people in all parts of the world, God becoming human is common enough. Even if the fulfillment of these aspirations was something wholly beyond imagination, the very thrust of them says a lot about human nature and the human quest for some participation in God. The first reaction to the discovery that many of our fundamental religious truths do not merely echo, but have close counterparts in other religions, even in what we call false religions, produced a kind of disillusionment. It seemed that our faith, too, was just another dream. Christmas is but an updated primitive celebration of the winter solstice. Later it came home to us that our faith is rather strongly affirmed by these spiritual insights, many of them profound, that far from being alien to human nature, our faith is instead wholly consistent, consonant with it. So much so that we can say that if the impossible were possible, we would have invented the faith had it not been revealed.

So, the virgin birth, Jesus as God and human, his death for us at our hands, his resurrection from the dead, his ascension into heaven—all these call us after him. These realities are not diminished because they were the mystical yearnings of much of mankind, the dreams and desires of the human soul; they are rather the more strongly emphasized. That these, our divine mysteries, are rooted in history and are not poetic figments of imagination becomes their ultimate distinction and greatest power. They happened. It is all true.

If, then, the dualities so common in our thinking—God and humanity, heaven and hell, time and eternity, body and soul, male and female, left and right, interior and exterior—are without difficulty accepted as terms for revelation too, how much more amazing is it that the most sublime of religious truths, the Holy Trinity, should also have been stumbled on in some way by the human mind long before the truth was fully known, for the idea of a triune God is not unknown in other religious cultures This truth, too, satisfies something in us: has an appeal touching something deep down.

Is it possible to consider how a people might have wondered whether trinity was not found in God.

Duality leads to union, as we know well enough, and then this union is something new, a third. Body and soul form the human; you are not body, you are not soul, nor body and soul together, but a new third, the human.

Vision is not possible without duality. Having two eyes is essential if one is to know distance and perspective. Only two ears make possible a hearing that is complete, that takes in the whole range of sound. You cannot by sound locate a plane flying overhead if you have only one ear, for you lack the coordinates. Thus even our hearing and our vision, though dual, bring a third into being because the fruit of sight and sound is the exact point to which they lead. Sound is stereophonic, that is, three dimensional, embodied. Sight is stereoscopic, three dimensional, two plus one.

Fullness, the whole, takes two hands. We sense this when we grasp something with both hands. We then feel we have a hold on our subject, in many senses. One hand extended to another is a commercial deal, a military pact, something civil. But such a handshake is not an act of love. If we love someone we use two hands, two arms. When Paul VI embraced Athenagoras, he did not merely shake hands with him, like at the Rotary or Kiwanis Club. Two leads to three. Two hands make a relation, something new, a third.

The fruit of human love is the child, the new third born of love. And indeed, within the person, celibate or espoused, the union of opposites within brings about the development and full flower of the mature person neither male nor female, but Christ- like, androgynous, the full person, the new third.

Pondering these notions, as humans have done since time began, could well enough lead to a consideration of a God, sole, singular, who generated another and in union with him knew a third who was one with them, as in sight, in sound, in touch, in love, in maturity.

We sometimes think that the whole mystery of the Trinity is so profound a truth—it is the most profound in Christianity— that consideration of it is best left to professional theologians. Yet it was monks who first celebrated it liturgically. Even people who did not know revelation have seen in threeness something fascinating and divine. Frank Sheed, who for years preached to all comers in the open air in parks and squares and street corners, said that more questions were asked about the Holy Trinity than any other subject.

This feast, made an observance by the whole church by Pope John XXII in 1334, is a call to us to probe this holy mystery. The singular is so often dual, and one duality so often leads to a new third which is in turn fruit of the two found in the one.

It is in Christ that we not only contemplate this sublime mystery, but truly enter into it, share in it, are adopted as children of the Father in Christ by the Spirit given us. If the Christian experience, rather than theological investigation, is what we seek, this is the awareness brought home to us today, why we as monks celebrate it. Through Christ in the Spirit we come before the Father. As sight, sound, a touch, human love, maturity, so we: in Christ, by the Spirit, to the Father.

O holy and undivided Trinity, one God, the Father, Son and Holy Spirit, to whom be glory and honor forever and ever. Amen.

10

FACING THE DEVIL ❧

In their synagogue just then there was a man possessed by
an unclean spirit, and it shouted, 'What do you want with
us, Jesus of Nazareth? Have you come to destroy us? I know
who you are: the Holy One of God.' But Jesus said sharply,
'Be quiet! Come out of him!' And the unclean spirit threw
the man into convulsions and with a loud cry went out of
him. The people were so astonished that they started asking
each other what it all meant. 'Here is a teaching that is new'
they said 'and with authority behind it: he gives orders even to
unclean spirits and they obey him.' And his reputation rapidly
spread everywhere, through all the surrounding Galilean
countryside. (Mark 1:23–28)

A long while ago, when I was in seminary, there was a di-
abolical possession at the place. A woman was brought
to the guesthouse from Iowa in the hope that some of
the priests would be able to deal with the situation despite the
fact that the case had been widely publicized and a number of
attempts had been to date unavailing. One stalwart Father took
the devil on, but met his match in short order. Once the Father
had launched into his business, the woman, or the devil, as the
case may be began in a shrieking, mocking voice to expose all
the priest's past sins. That was the end of it for him.

I was reminded of that by this morning's gospel and the
confrontation of good and evil that was much the result of Jesus
appearing on the scene. Nothing provokes evil as much as the
presence of good, the sign of contradiction.

I do not think it takes a sinless person to confront the evil
one. And I do not think exorcisms can be performed only by
the guiltless, for who of us is without sin? But I do think that in

39

a confrontation of good and evil we must deal with realities and not with make-believe. An exorcist, even one who has known sin, can face the evil one, but can face it only from the basis of the real self. The father of lies recognizes sham.

Our recent exposure to Gandhi and our thoughts on nonviolence come into question here. Most monks are well acquainted with non-violence and civil disobedience and non-cooperation. They are the age-old tools against a host of evils: the false self, the worldly ego, the acquired persona, the veneer personality, the front we put on.

In trying to cope with a strongly held position it is of no use whatever to assert one's self, to take a strong stand, to make a firm act of the will in some express way or other. This is simply to reassert the self we seek to destroy. A religious *persona* is no better than a worldly one; in fact it is worse.

Refusal to accept, unwillingness to go along with, resentment against someone or something we do not like, passive aggression against an unaccepted condition, the prolonged pout and the perduring non-compliance are absurd, and so is anyone who thinks they do any good at all. They are the work of the worldly ego. This is to walk around in circles and wonder why we do not get anywhere in the spiritual life.

Our assault is not against someone, something, outside us, but someone, something, within. Against this power only the non-violent will succeed. To use violence against tyrants is to fight with tyrants on their own terms and so to be overcome by them. There is no winning at that. To unseat an occupying power one must use a different tactic, the tactic of non-violence, non-cooperation, civil disobedience. Refuse to take the false self seriously, do not fear it, or respect it, or make anything of it.

It is obedience that teaches us this, not any obedience, but obedience in and with and for Jesus Christ. Only obedience will break the strangle-hold that the false self has on us. In accord with the teaching of Saint Benedict we move along in this until our obedience enters into our relations even with each other so that brother obeys brother, including brother wind and sister rain and brother ice and sister snow. We accept what comes and tolerate what the day brings, since our morning offering is not the one- sided gift of ourselves and all we do, but is also a willingness to receive whatever comes our way. Only through such obedience will we shake off the tyrant and usurper, and attain to freedom and to joy.

Until we have moved that far along, God is not going to take us very seriously and the devil certainly is not; God because we would never respond to the divine action in us, the devil because we are not free enough to have any stature.

God works through the free, and it is the free who can cope with evil, for it is certain that in the face of such good, evil will show its face. There will be conflict. It was predicted. But because the good person is free of falsity and is possessed by the spirit of Christ and utterly possessed by him, evil has no power. A houseful of obedient monks is a terror to demons and the delight of the Spirit of God. The disobedient are dull and boring to God and demons alike.

The obedient do not need the testimony of the demons that they are sinners, nor are they frightened of it. They know what they are well enough. But they know the mercy of God, too, and have therefore the joy of the children of God. They know exactly what Gandhi was talking about, and apply it not to the political world—though they could—but to the world of the spirit. That is the area where Gandhi was most effective, the root of his external success. So we become agents of good in the world by reason of being possessed by God. It is worth the try. Otherwise we are not worth the candle we hold or held yesterday. Amen.

11

FORGIVENESS ❦

I do not believe there is anything quite as important as the love of mercy. We need to return to this truth time without end, for the reason that our need of mercy is so great and our tendency to depart from it so strong.

Elemental in our understanding of mercy is the basic role of forgiveness. I ask you, can any greater harm come to the soul than by want of forgiveness?

Let us think of forgiveness in three ways: forgiveness of God; forgiveness of our neighbor; forgiveness of ourselves. We may not perhaps be ready to see our need to forgive God, yet it is not at all unlikely that there is a large place for it in our hearts. There are many things in our life, in life around us, that are very difficult, if not impossible, to understand: war, pestilence, hunger, poverty, earthquake, tornado—any tragedy on a massive level. While we do not admit to blaming God for these things, they arouse in the human heart a log of wondering why these things are, why there is such colossal human misery quite apparently beyond human control and quite obviously within God's. What sort of God tolerates such horrors? Theological explanations are all well and good, but when we confront these horrors in the concrete, the explanations tend to appear weak and futile, unable to curb a sense of resentment and even outrage against God. Nor is this rare. It is no small thing to maintain a faith in the loving God in the face of such overwhelming facts of life.

On a personal level we confront a similar situation, but on a much smaller scale. The smaller scale does not mean that the suffering seems much less, for even global disaster is experienced only on the personal, individual level. Why am I who I am and why am I the way I am? Why are the components that have gone into my history so often poor and inadequate? In terms of my body, my mind, my soul, my size and shape, my childhood, my youth—indeed all my history: why are they what they are?

Without our even being aware of it, we hide in our deepest depths some resentment against God for making us as we are, our history what it is. This does not mean that we are a bundle of resentment, though some people are, but rather that some resentment may well be present, obvious to us once in a while, maybe in a passing moment of insight.

So it seems necessary to forgive God. Sometimes, from a human point of view, we hold something against God, we have an argument. We need to face this and to answer it with genuine forgiveness. If we do not, we are bound to have surface in our lives, early or late, a bitterness that may sour many of our years, the more so if we do not know the source. It is very possible—I will not quite say likely—that we have wandering around in our own depths some sense of umbrage at the way God has treated us. I think it rather futile to try to come up with explanations, for they are not deep enough or divine enough to quell the sense of our fury at God for the way things are with us.

Forgiveness is an act of faith rooted in Christ. It is not explanation. In the presence of something we cannot for the life of us understand, and which is and has been the source of anguish and suffering, forgiveness for Christ's sake is the only way out. It is a superb act of faith in God. It is no small thing to forgive God what God has done to us. This is to speak all too humanly, yet human we are and we experience God in a human way—here below in any case.

Forgiveness of our neighbor is a companion to forgiveness of God. It is of enormous importance. It is utterly necessary that we have absolutely nothing against anyone, living or dead, that we forgive all wrong done to us, literally, totally, and from the heart. And if we do not, if we are not in such a state, then we must ask God continually for grace, a grace that will assuredly be given.

We sometimes entertain the notion that it is not inconsistent with Christian love to maintain an unforgiving attitude toward those who have done us wrong. This lack of forgiveness may not be explicit, yet it can be very much alive in our hearts and may extend way back to our childhood, for it is by no means rare for children to suffer grievous wrong at the hands of their elders, wrongs which often leave deep wounds, which are somehow kept open by an unforgiving Spirit.

Almost everyone at some stage of life experiences injustice or shameful treatment, and I do not exclude life in religion. I do not mean misunderstandings, or a blunder, or some passing human weakness, but outright wrong, evil. It is a normal human response to withhold forgiveness, the more so when we, our work, our reputation, have been shattered by it. We may then feel entitled to keep alive within us a sense of wounded justice, and we may feel quite right in doing so, and by some adjustment of mental attitudes reconcile this with our faith. I do not refer to external behavior—for we may carry on here with accustomed courtesy in day to day exchange—but to the bottom of the heart where unforgiveness is kept constant. This is a dreadful mistake. I say mistake, for if we keep alive such an attitude, we surely do not think it a sin, though objectively it undoubtedly is. But if we see it as a mistake we may be able to see clearly that it is a sin.

When we are young, we can carry on with an unforgiving heart without apparent harm. But as we grow older, this changes. Why is that? Because we are less active or that our activity takes less from us than it did before? That it becomes more routine, and leads us to discover that this focus of bitterness in our depths has become a kind of cancer that has spread. It may cloud our whole outlook, manifest itself in daily life in certain circumstances that are just right. A genuine bitterness may touch the whole of our lives: what we say, what we think, what we do. And the unforgiving attitude that was once confined to a specific instance becomes common, and a whole life is embittered.

This too is not rare. People think they can confine lack of forgiveness to a particular event, a special case. You cannot, not in the end. Forgiveness is total. There can be no exceptions. No matter how justified the case, lack of forgiveness is never justified. And you cannot get away with it. We bring on ourselves a terrible judgment, for every time we say the *Our Father* the agreement is struck: forgive as we forgive. If we do not forgive, the evil remains in us and can ultimately destroy us. When we are unforgiving we must pray continually for the gift of mercy.

People are perhaps more unforgiving of themselves than of God or neighbor. This runs deep in humankind and is ultimately rooted in original sin, the subtle awareness that we are touched with evil, are unworthy of love, deserve to be condemned. Sometimes a wrongly or mistakenly applied spirituality can give this lack of proper self-esteem such emphasis that one's basic confidence is undermined. I read not long ago in an American religious journal that self condemnation is common among religious. There is a real need for mercy and compassion, indeed forgiveness, toward our own self. One says, 'I can never forgive myself' for some wrong done and yet such a statement is wholly unchristian. One must forgive oneself as one must also forgive others. A merciless condemnation of one's self for faults, failings, weakness, is heartless. In no sense is it humility, for humility is truth, and the truth is that no matter what we have done, what we are, we abide in God's forgiving love. No one denies that we are gross sinners, but the truth also insists that our sins are forgiven and we are loved.

There is no sense denying the darkness of despair that makes its presence felt in our hearts. This was what drove Martin Luther, after many years as a monk, to purge himself of any program of good works to rely on faith and faith alone. So too the good works of our own life, however inadequate, however splendid they be, are not going to be enough to establish us in that trust in God which is the key to salvation and to inner peace.

A constant inner nagging, an unending belittling, a manner of blaming, reproaching, condemning ourselves without mercy, far from pleasing God, is an insult to God, for it presumes that our salvation and sanctification are our own doing, that if we beat our breast without mercy and drive on without stinting, God will eventually do what God should do and so justify us.

An emphasis on self-condemnation may indicate how much we need to grow in faith and trust in God. If we show mercy we will see it, give it; also to ourselves. For one of your neighbors is you and if we are bidden earnestly to show mercy to others, among those others is you. And oddly enough, though it is said of this one or that, 'He was hard on himself and kind to others', I do not believe it. Someone who is hard on himself will be hard on others; one is merciful or one isn't. You cannot be merciful to one and hateful to another, nor love one neighbor and condemn another. Mercy is all or none. If you condemn yourself, you condemn your neighbor's brother or sister.

It is good to reflect on these truths. Being unforgiving toward God is not rare. Being unforgiving toward a neighbor is much more common. And I think being unforgiving to one's self most common of all.

We must enter the realm of mercy and dwell in its happy precincts, mercy received and mercy given being the coin of the realm by which the wealth of God's love becomes as riches available to all.

Forgive us our sins as we forgive those who sin against us. Amen.

12

OBEDIENCE ❧

Jesus and his disciples left for the villages round Casesarea Philippi. On the way he put this question to his disciples, 'Who do people say I am?' (Mark 8:27)

When I was a novice, the second time—for being a slow learner I have usually had to do things twice before I catch on—Father Louis used to give out the work every morning. He did it personally and he did it with care. Most of the years I have been in Gethsemani we have been building, either tearing down or putting up. Most of it is hard labor. But, he would assign other things too: work in the woods, in the yard, and, for me, worst of all, typing, typing his manuscripts on mimeograph stencils. I type about as well as I play the piano. Forget it. But I was the only one who could do anything on a stencil. Not all my days were good days in the novitiate and on one of the worst he assigned me to typing. 'Father Matthew, you will type.' And I said, 'No, I won't.' Then the same request and the same response. He waited. Then he said it again, without the hint of a smile. I paused and then I said, 'OK, I type.' And he said, 'That was the old man in you; he is not dead yet.' I do believe my monastic vocation was at stake at that moment. Once more and he would have said, 'You will be happier where you came from.' I kid you not.

Christ had a similar confrontation with Peter this morning. And Christ was more pointed in his remarks than my Father Louis was. I daresay he was rather angry. With cutting directness he spoke those famous words, 'Get behind me, Satan'. What he meant was, 'You are not with it, Peter. You do not get it. You are operating from a worldly ego, an earthly ego. You think with your mind. You are being reasonable, logical.

That's not enough for the kingdom. It operates on different principles, from another point of view, entirely. The ego has to go, Peter. Go deeper. Go further down where God dwells in you, in the very heart of you where the true you are and where God is one with you. Give up the world of delusion and make believe.'

But Christ put it more neatly, 'Get behind me, Satan.' I know of no lesson more difficult to learn, nor one more essential to following Christ.

Because it is difficult, it is often misunderstood, misinterpreted, even perverted. That is a way of getting around it. We know the gate is narrow and road rough that leads to life, so we think all we need is to make life hard and tough and then we will have it. As if it were that easy. Who does not know how penance and toughness and fasting and denial can swell the ego instead of killing it. Or, since he said the way is easy and the burden is light, we think then that joy is the heart of it. Just be jolly and bright and we will dance our way into the kingdom, full of sunshine and merriment in the merry Jesus. A word with you? That is not it. We know too that work and discipline and hours of prayer are essential, and so they are, and yet we know from our own experience that this is not enough.

What do you tell people who are afflicted with terrible suffering? How do you make God sound good to people whose lives have been devastated by disaster through no fault of their own. Good people, who lose their children, who have no work, whose wives run off with a lout. Things like that happen every day to good people, not to mention those who by piling their own confused sins end to end make an enormous mess of their lives. Tragedy is as common as rain in this good country. Travel a bit and you would see worse and more.

Nothing shatters faith as much as suffering, deserved and undeserved. Perhaps more when deserved. And there is a lot of both. Have you noticed?

Christ said the pain in his life was the will of the Father. And that is what we tell people: the will of god. God's will be done.

But the mess we are in is a mess we created. This is all our doing. It need not have been, but it is. It is our doing, a community action.

The way out of it was for Christ to become one of us and to share it all. Like us, he was to see it as God's will. So the world is redeemed. Doing his will we undo the damage of our own.

You and I want to be part of that great work. Thus it will be suffering and death for you as it is for everyone else. The more profoundly you enter into that, the more profoundly you share in the great work of Christ and the more profound your love of humankind. People all around us suffer and die. With Christ, we join them, on purpose.

In the face of that, cultivating a personality, developing our talents, finding fulfillment, achieving happiness is absurd. That is why Father Louis told us novices to eat the soup. Like it, lump it, eat it. If you cannot manage that, why are you getting into this life? You will never make it. Later, when you are professed, you can skip the soup.

Who are your heroes? Who are your famous people? Whom do you praise? It tells a lot about you. Who is your favorite abbot? I will tell you who mine is. He is my hero, my Christ figure. He was handsome, intelligent, graced, eloquent, and he built the most beautiful Cistercian abbey in the country. In mid-term, mid-life, in hours of glory, he was struck down, removed from office for reasons unknown. He went into exile. He died years later in a far away abbey dreaming of return and reinstatement. But he was at peace. That is what I mean, this is what it means to redeem the world with Christ.

Do you want to attain such heights? It is easy. Go the way Christ went, the way of obedience, the only way. No one ever developed an ego being obedient. A house full of obedient monks is the glory of God. Otherwise it is a kindergarten.

It is said that after that terrible rebuke from Christ, Peter wept. He was to weep again. But, in the end, he learned. So can we. Amen.

13

Today This Scripture is Fulfilled ❧

Then he began to speak to them, 'This text is being fulfilled today even as you listen'. And he won the approval of all, and they were astonished by the gracious words that came from his lips.

They said, 'This is Joseph's son, surely?' But he replied, 'No doubt you will quote me the saying, "Physician, heal yourself" and tell me, "We have heard all that happened in Capernaum, do the same here in your own countryside'". And he went on, 'I tell you solemnly, no prophet is ever accepted in his own country.'

'There were many widows in Israel, I can assure you, in Elijah's day, when heaven remained shut for three years and six months and a great famine raged throughout the land, but Elijah was not sent to any one of these: he was sent to a widow at Zarephath, a Sidonian town. And in the prophet Elisha's time there were many lepers in Israel, but none of these was cured, except the Syrian, Naaman.'

When they heard this everyone in the synagogue was enraged. They sprang to their feet and hustled him out of the town; and they took him up to the brow of the hill their town was built on, intending to throw him down the cliff, but he slipped through the crowd and walked away.
(Luke 4:21–30)

Last Sunday's gospel incident and this Sunday's are two sides of a whole, two slopes of the same mountain, one dark and one light. For the verse that began today's excerpt was the ending of last week's, 'Today this scripture has been fulfilled in your hearing'. What led up to this dictum was positive and light; what followed after it, dark and negative. The verse is some sort of fulcrum, a line of division, the balance point of two weights.

It may perhaps be something of a shock when we first realize that the Good News is not always good news to everyone. It is bad news to some. If the feet of the one bearing good tidings of peace over the mountain are blessed, blessed too are the feet bringing tidings of war—for some.

> *The Spirit of the Lord is upon me*
> *because he has anointed me to preach good news*
> *to the poor.*
> *He has sent me to proclaim release to captives*
> *and recovery of sight to the blind,*
> *to set at liberty those who are oppressed,*
> *to proclaim the acceptable time of the Lord.*

So run the words of the prophet. One would think that the day of their fulfillment was a good day. I have news for you. It was a bad day for a lot of people.

When Christ stood up, unrolled the book and read from it, rolled it up again and sat down, looked into the faces of his townsmen and said, 'Today this scripture is fulfilled in your hearing', he most certainly knew what was coming.

He knew that they would not have it, that what he said was not welcome. That he was not welcome. The more he said, the more obvious it became. The more he spoke, the worse things got. In a sense, it would have been better had he not gone to the synagogue at all. Or, if he had gone, had not accepted the invitation to speak. And if he spoke, not spoken on this particular text. As it was, he could not have done worse. Would it be appropriate to say he lacked prudence? And not content with that, he went on to speak of yet another prophecies, to detail the very response his neighbors were now making to him. In the end he was barely able to escape with his life.

Yet, if you are a quiet observer of your own heart, none of this will seem too strange to you. And, I might add, one of the points of living apart in a context of quiet is precisely to be able to observe.

It is not fair, of course, to jump to the conclusion that, because I find in my own heart unsavory reactions to good, the same must be true of you. Let that pass.

Resentment in the presence of good is probably a logical reaction for someone who feels not much favored by the high and mighty, human or divine. In other words poor people can hardly be blamed if they are jealous of the rich.

Sinners often respond negatively to virtue. Goodness is not universally loved. We can observe this easily enough in children in whom passion is sometimes exhibited with a candor that amazes their elders. For the sweetest little children can be overcome with envy or spite or fury when another outshines or outperforms or is preferred to them.

Adults with a little practice, can keep their responses plausible enough. Yet most humans are full of foibles, are blemished and marred. Human virtue is very limited. It is generally easy to justify our abuse. In the presence of undoubted patience we need only remind others that we have seen days when their patience was in no way evident. Someone who is generous today was stingy yesterday. If the present pope is a saint, past popes have been monsters.

What ruins this, however, is Christ. Here was someone totally good, yet totally rejected. He was not merely driven out of his land as a child, driven out of his home town as an adult, but all his life he was haunted and hunted and hated, and in the end done to death with a viciousness that is appalling. Yet even a common crook hanging next to him on a cross knew as well as everyone else that the man was without blame.

Here is a mystery worth pondering, which is one reason, I suppose, that this story is spread over two Sundays. We are to live with it a long time. Nothing will bring out the evil in us as fast and as effectively as the presence of good. This is one of the reasons we fear God. Is it healthy to get too close to God? Is it safe to be intimate with the divine? Or, if you do get close, is it not best to keep talking? And perhaps wisest not to ask for comment?

A woman with an afflicted child, a child tormented with demons or born not quite right, will defend the fruit of her womb with a heat that makes the bold tremble if she hears the slightest ill said of her child. Because we are an afflicted people who bear the marks of a dreadful past, it is no wonder we are tormented when we come into the presence of supreme loveliness and beauty.

Though I do not know about you, I wonder if I would not have been one of the people of his village who drove Jesus to the edge of the hill in the hope of shoving him over it. It is sometimes very bitter to be poor. And yet, we have a God who loves us more than any earthly mother could love a malformed child.

Believing this is the gist of being a Christian. It continues to be, it also seems, the most arduous and the most worthy of all the works of God. God help us all to do it. Thus this scripture may be fulfilled in our hearing. And in God's. And that is Good News indeed. Amen.

14

THE RAISING OF LAZARUS ❧

In the course of our lives we generally do the same thing,
say the same thing, many times over and in many different
ways. But the basic thrust is there, an identical emphasis
and a common modality. So true is this that if we discover our
own or another's fundamental melody, we shall have the key to
our own story, the identifying phrase of a person's song.

Sun signs from popular astrology are an attempt at this. So
are the Sufi symbols [Enneagram] that the Franciscan friar
introduced to us—for many of us had not known of them—an
exercise in discovering some sort of consistent pattern in the
human so persistent and so persuasive that a person's behavior
becomes understandable, even predictable.

Pious legend has it that Jesus as a child at play used to fashion
little crosses. The legend may be a bit cloying, the point is not.
Jesus was associated with the cross all his life. At certain times
this became striking. Today's gospel (John 11) is such a time.
Here, just a short while before his actual passion, Jesus acts
out in another his death and his rising from the dead. Rather
than spoil a good thing by subjecting it to my comment, I limit
myself to three items I suggest you think about, if you've a mind
to: tender love, apparent indifference, and feminine presence.

The tender love of the Lord for Lazarus and for his two
sisters is well known. What I marvel at is how little we imitate
it. If I should say to you, 'the brother I love is sick', you would
not, I bet you, know to whom I refer. Is there anyone here
I could refer to as 'the monk you love'? We are such a cold
lot. I do not mean me and you and monks especially. I mean

Americans, North Atlantic people. But you know as well as I do that things change. The northern hemisphere is warming up. The movement can be recognized clearly in places like a monastery. Are you aware of that? Do you know that love grows stronger, becomes more evident, more vocal? To be sure, it is only a beginning, but it has begun. It is a massive ground swell of change, detected early in places like this, but not only here. Some of you don't like it, or resist it, or may even be ignorant of it. It matters little. Your not knowing changes nothing, your resisting it is like holding your hand up to stop the wind or the rain.

Are you aware of the growth that is occurring in the contemplative life, far outstripping anything we have known for centuries? All the signs are there. Can you read them? Be, I pray, as shrewd as the leaders of the people in the gospel today, who knew exactly what Jesus was saying in the raising of Lazarus.

There is no love that will not vary tenderness with indifference. How else can I know that you love me? If you cannot tolerate pain you will not be able to tolerate love. Jesus let Lazarus die and he need not have done so. He does this and even worse things. 'It need not have been' is a frightful thing to have to say to God. I think, as monks, you need to sink very deep into this bottomless mystery. No one is spared, you know. But those who think of themselves as close to Jesus ought to be able to catch the theme, detect it in the midst of much other music.

Neither love nor pain will be anything to you without woman. It is not just that you were born of woman. In simple cultures a woman always assisted at childbirth, and at death. The same woman, often enough. There a birth, here a death: the primal events. Women were very close to Jesus, in birth and death, and to Lazarus. Women prepared the Lord's body for the resurrection. Not men. Women were at the foot of the cross, as was his mother. Not men. The men had long since taken off, save one, the disciple he loved.

If you as a monk cannot relate to woman, how are you like Jesus? If you do not relate to the woman within you, you are wasting time. You cheat the people for whom God made you a monk. If you do not know pain you will never know Jesus. If there is no one around whom you love, I wonder where you are. We need tender love, apparent pain, the woman's touch.

You look back in your life and you see these three there time and again. They keep coming back in many ways. But it is always the same melody, a song that lingers on, dies, and returns. It is your Enneagram, your sign. You. Amen.

15

In Touch With His Father's Love ♣

A story appears in the *Butterfly*, a newsletter issued by the ministry to the sick and elderly by the Sisters of Loretto in Nerinx, Kentucky. Lou Little, when coaching at Georgetown, had a player with little talent, but his spirit was an inspiration to the team. Although he rarely played, the boy asked to start in a game, just after his father had died. The coach agreed, fully expecting to take him out after the first few plays. The boy played so well that he stayed in for the whole game. Later, when the coach praised the young man for his excellent plays, the boy explained that his father had been blind. "This is the first time he ever saw me play!"

The story is very fitting for this time of All Saints and All Souls. The relationship we have to those especially close to us is, of course, a very deep one. It is not nonsense to agree with the young man that his dead father was indeed watching him play. It is a good idea these November days to recall that we too will one day be among the dead. Let us assist them if they need our prayer, rejoice with them if they be in the kingdom, and be closer to them than we ever were on earth.

There is also a link between this story and the gospel of this morning in Matthew 23:1–12. Jesus makes light of religious leaders who set great store in the appearance of things. Looking good is a common enough preoccupation, and it is by no means rare among people committed to religion. Jesus spotted it in his day, as we see. It is, after all, always needful to edify, and sometimes edification can take the form of pretense. If you do not have the wherewithal, you pretend you do.

Jesus pointed out the absurdity of imagining that marks of honor of whatever kind are going to add anything to what you already are. He does not, I believe, fault honor and places of honor. He does not fault piety and works of piety. Perhaps he would not even mention our having the best seats in the synagogue, should he appear in our balcony some Sunday morning. Perhaps. What does annoy him is the assumption that doing any of these things makes us better people.

Wealthy people put on airs because they think money makes them better than others. I have news for them. Intelligent people tend to think they are better because they are smart. They are not, I assure you. Handsome people, especially men, take their superiority for granted, most of them. One of the most amusing sections of the *New York Times* is the society page of wedding announcements. Elegant brides and grooms spell out their pedigrees like those of well-bred horses or cows.

We are all fearful people. Monks too. We hide our fears in so many ways, timid lot that we are, behind arrogance or stubbornness or laziness or indifferences. Who is more persistent than a timid monk? Who more intolerant? More diffident in choir? If the Pharisees wore their phylacteries wide and their fringes long, we do pretty well, too. I work in the tailor shop. This is no big thing. It is no sin to be human. But it is a sin to be blind to what is human and to what is divine as well. That is something else again.

It was because his father loved him that the boy played so well. He had a loving eye on him. Through death the father entered into a communion with the son he never had before and could not have because he was blind. It is through the passion and death of Jesus that we enter into a communion with him that we never had before, or could have had, for we were blind to the love of God for us, the love God still has, will always have. That is what matters. Now our endeavor is not to prove something, win something, gain something. It is rather response. It is because we are loved that we perform, that we play a good game. Something else entirely. The boy's game never got off the ground as long as he was playing on a level without vision. But once his eyes were opened he was free to be good. Real good. There is nothing unique about being timid, then. Common as rain on Sunday. The most common obstacle in the spiritual life. What is a blunder, and Jesus tells us that today, is to cover it with something that will never do. You have to get to the root of the matter.

The young man never got anywhere as a player while timidity cramped his style. Once he was in touch with his father's love through the vision that faith gives, everything in him was set free and he played as he had never played before. It is this same faith that will set us free of the life of pretense and cover-up, hanging tough because it looks good.

You cannot live without an awareness that others are looking. To try to do this is silly, simply another pretense. But we do not live, do not play, because they are looking. We play for the love of it. Love is the meaning of it all. And since love is a communal thing, a community business, I want you around. What kind of game is it with nobody looking on? And how can you possibly play a good game unless your eyes are on your lover, the lover's on you? Amen.

16

ALL SOULS DAY ❧

The other night you are on your way to Compline and you decide to go around outside the rear of the church because it is a wild night and worth sampling. Heavy rain and a splendid wind tears down the last of the leaves. A perfect night for the dark end of the year, for All Saints and for All Souls. And as you come to the door and reach out to put your hand to the clasp, you notice a light down by the juniper where Father Louis lies buried. You look again and there bright and clear, no murk, no mist, stands Brother Zachary, cowl blowing in the wind. He looks right at you, that Mona Lisa smile on his lips, and bows to you. For maybe a whole minute you are together and then as quick as that he is gone and there is nothing but the dark and the wind and the rain and you standing there about to open the door.

You go into Compline, only Compline is a bit different for you that night. Maybe the next day you see someone, your confessor, the abbot; maybe that night already. And he will tell you what Father Louis told us when we were novices: nothing to fuss over. No great thing. Perfectly natural. Nothing to marvel at. Make nothing of it. Thank God for it. It's like a good dream. Maybe your faith is weak and needs bolstering. Just make very sure you do not coax this sort of thing. No fetching up this kind of experience. Very dangerous. Very bad.

People used to come to me when I was in the South Pacific and beg me almost with tears to help them. And what was I to help them with? They wanted to see their dead. They did not *think* I saw the dead. They *knew* I did. I was the holy man. I lived alone on a hill. I prayed. Out back there was the cemetery for the early missionaries which I visited every day. They used to see their dead too, they said, in times past. But they don't anymore. Why? Well, their lives are too distracted now. They can travel about, which they could never do before. There are radio and news and money and stores and strangers and lots of exciting things going on. So they have lost what they had before. And they worry about it. Maybe their dead are angry. Maybe something is wrong. They miss what was.

Primitive indeed. But right on, for all that. You know how westerners differ from primitives? You know how moderns differ from the people of the ages of faith? Westerners, moderns, have lost contact with their depths. They are no longer in communion with themselves. This leads to disease. And moderns are very sick with this disease.

One reason why monasteries exist now and have existed before is that they set up an environment where it is possible to be healthy, to be normal. It is really necessary to do this, for it is not easy to be healthy when everyone around you is sick, not easy to be normal when all about you are mad.

What a monastery does is create a climate in which communion with the world of the spirit is easy and normal. Natural. A primitive village is like that. Celtic Ireland was like that. The Ages of Faith, so called, were like that. And we aim to be like that too.

All the elements of the monastic life make up the total picture, the habitat. First of all, a high regard for Jesus Christ and the effort to make him the center of everything. And then there is the matter of realism, of contact with nature, with work, with people, on a real level, not on a level of make believe, of pretense, contact not by way of competition and aggression, but by way of love, of cooperation. A monastery should be a place of beauty, for beauty is elemental. We cannot live without beauty, the beauty of worship, of context, of style, the beauty of tenderness and care, of thoughtfulness, of composure, and, most of all, I guess, the beauty of quiet. Quiet is the most precious commodity of all, that rare quality so long since banished from human haunts. Without quiet there is no pondering. Without pondering there is no contact with the depths. And without contact with the depths we perish.

People perish all around us, day by day. They are overwhelmed by darkness in the midst of a world of so much and so much good. So many good people are overwhelmed. And whence the darkness? The darkness is from within. When the depths are ignored, when the unconscious is repressed, it backs up and then one day it explodes, and gets its revenge. For our depths, you see, are not only good. Sure, they are good. But they are like the human self, also evil. The good and the evil within must be faced in Jesus Christ. Otherwise things happen without our knowing why.

Whence comes the madness that marks so much of our times, the awful movements that swept over the earth, the terrifying trends, the hideous gospels that are spread everywhere and work so much harm? Whence, if not from our depths, evil easily and blandly embraced, espoused, advocated, propagated. I spare you calling them by name. You know them all. And words are of no avail against these demons.

We laugh at the primitive Celts, the ignorant Irish. We smile at the weird ways of primitive peoples. But say this much for them, my wise brother, say this much: at least they deal with the powers within, which is more than our world does. Our world denies we have anything within. And look at the consequences of our folly.

How needful it is then to have monasteries, real monasteries, not just men's clubs, not just places of competent work and estimable liturgy and adequate learning and decent people. We need monasteries in which the depths are met in Jesus Christ, in which good is blessed and evil cursed. This does not take exceptional people, only human, normal persons, who know the rain and feel the wind, who know darkness and the silence of the night, who can abide with quiet and know the beauty of a simple way of living, without clamor and din, without noise and confusion, without constant distraction and the unending input that overwhelms a poor human.

Lest the world perish.

Not that we need to see the dead. We have our faith and faith is enough for us. But seeing the dead is only one aspect of our dealings with inner realities. It is only thus that faith can survive, for religion dies when there is no longer contact with the depths within. It is good to be an introvert, for then it comes easily. It is good to have a strong relation to the woman within, for then the tension is there that is so creative. And it is good to know that nothing is as fitting as listening, nothing as rewarding as docility, nothing as commanding as obedience, for obedience curbs selfishness and assertion and arrogance and pride, that host of enemies that lay waste the spirit.

Today we think of the dead. Their brief moment is now over. They are now in eternity. Now we have our brief moment here. We came yesterday, are here today, will be gone tomorrow. Let that brief moment be spent in communion with the whole of life so that we will not have lived in vain.

The whimsical smile of Brother Zachary implies that.

17

A Heart of Stone ❧

'I tell you, if these were silent, the very stones would cry out.' If 'these'—that is to say, 'my disciples were silent', seems to be what we are concerned with here. The human heart. The stones describe the human heart. Stones make up the fabric of houses, walls, walk-ways, road ways. It is their hardness that makes them fit for such things, their stability and endurance.

Christ here does not fault the stones around him. He faults the human heart that has taken on the nature of stone, not its perdurance and its stability so much as its hardness.

Here comes the Lord into his city, the Messiah into his Father's house, the Redeemer into the midst of his people. It is a moment of triumph and of victory. It is no hour for silent repression. Now is the time for exuberance and joy.

We may be sure, however, that not all who were witness to these events were vocal in their enthusiasm. Some were grim and kept their mouths shut, their lips tight. They found nothing to get excited about in all that was going on before them. Christ knew pain at the hardness of heart that was palpable, harder than stone.

Though purity of heart is often presented as the most appropriate ideal for the monk, I am not too sure we understand the term in its best sense. Unhappily for us, purity may come to take on overtones of iciness, rigidity and severity. I believe I'd rather see your heart tender than pure, if it must be one or the other. I'd rather you were flesh than marble, rather gentle than tough. People strong on their principles frighten me. So does one sort of purity. Principles are abstractions. Human beings are not. They know little satisfaction when you hand them stones.

Entering this day into the passion and death and rising of Our Lord, walking into Holy Week and the summit of this year's history, we might well wonder where our hearts are and what we are like.

As professionally religious people we might assume, I think, that our hearts are more likely to be tough than tender. We only need to listen to the Gospel: it was the religious people who condemned Christ. The rabble outside the Law were his friends. If we do not note this and in some way take it to heart, then perhaps there is room for much misgiving. If, to the contrary, we realize that there is truth in the sentiment, maybe we can be saved after all.

Being tender of heart means being vulnerable. A surface that is not hard will show stains. Sinks and sink boards used to be wooden. Stainless steel, formica, or some other hard surface will not, as you know, absorb anything touching it. A formica heart means that things will not bother you: your brother's feelings, your neighbor's sorrow, the common good. You steel yourself against such things. Tough hearts love contention, thrive on it. Taking firm stands, announcing one's position with definition, standing up against one's abbot: these are things a stout heart does with ease, even with pride and self-assurance, finding a certain fitness in such behavior.

A hard heart, like a stainless steel sink, can take a lot of abuse and not show it. So can a terrazzo floor. In a community of some size, they make sense.

But, unfortunately, monastic life is not at its best when common sense is the norm. If common sense were our basic approach, would we be here?

And is it not absolutely essential to know, to experience, the propensity of the human heart to hardness? Still more, the propensity of the religious human heart to hardness? Not to know this is dangerous. Not to experience it is an awesome handicap.

Unless we have been driven to a positive insistence on a toughening of our hide, have we known what it is to be hurt, to be wounded, and so known the fruits of exposure and openness? We all gladly speak of openness, but few remain open very long for the reason that people will walk through an open door and bring all their misery with them. An open window invites everything borne on the wings of wind. Before long, the door is closed and the window shut.

A monastery, by way of its seclusion, its centeredness, its stability, is in truth the house of the open door, the vulnerable heart. That is why monks find it hard to stay there. And if they stay, they are tempted to harden their hearts. It is a matter of survival.

Every passion, every heavy breath, every storm that passes over the human landscape of our time will sweep through our own heart's cloister. We left the world, we did, yet we met it and know it here for the first time, here where we live at its center.

To live here is to know the human heart and the human landscape. The temptation to turn our back on this heart and this landscape, to betray our calling, this basic work, must be resisted, not by wills of steel and self-assertion and a masterful determination, but with eyes ever on the Lord. Christ heals us or we are not healed. Christ saves us or we are not saved. It is his gazing on us that warms us and makes us tender, drives from us the fear that makes us taut and tight. It is the gentleness of his look that frees us from the tension and the rigidity born of doubt.

Set free, then, we can sing with abandon, 'Hosanna to the Son David'. We will not be silent, but will cry out, 'Blessed is he who comes in the name of the Lord'. Lest the very stones shame us.

18

A Figure on the Beach ❧

O ne of the loveliest scenes in the New Testament—
and there are really a great many—surely must be
this scene on the lake shore.

> Simon Peter said, 'I'm going fishing'. They replied,
> 'We'll come with you'. They went out and got into the
> boat but caught nothing that night. (John 21:3–6)

If it were fiction, it would be easier to praise it. One would
call attention to the charming beginning, 'I am going fishing',
and, 'We'll come with you'. Then the disappointing night
with nothing caught, and the contrasting scene at dawn with
that mysterious figure on the beach over a fire with fish and
bread. And the call echoing over the quiet morning water, the
suggestion to try the other side, so often the best advice, so very
obvious and for that very reason turned down in our darkest
hours of failure. 'Try the other side.'

Typically impulsive, Peter responds to the sensitive John who
knew it was Jesus before anyone else did. It is a superb art. And
mind you, it is not a story. It is history. There is much more.
Yet I would make but one point with you, hopefully expecting
you to take it along this morning.

I read in a report of a house council meeting, in fact I was
there, that maybe as many as a third of you do not hear what
is said from this podium. I told someone that you are very
nice about it. You do not betray the fact that you do not get
a word. So I feel like the blooming apple tree in the girth,

full of sweet blossoms, only a fraction of which will ever end as fruit. A splendid waste of God's prodigality. But basically a matter of communication. Blossoms are not enough; they must be fructified. And this is what I think on in the gospel portion. Christ said to Peter, 'Do you love me?' On this blossom let us dwell a moment, draw sweetness, communicate, bear fruit.

What sort of men are these? When was the last time you walked down the beach and met a group of men and heard them asking one another, 'Do you love me?' It is hardly enough to say that this is different. What do we mean different? We mean it belongs in a stained-glass window? It belongs in an illuminated lectionary because Jesus is God? He can't talk like that to Peter because Peter was a pope? But I thought that what Jesus did we are supposed to do. You know, turn the cheek, walk another mile, give your shirt, forgive seventy times seven times, wash each other's feet, love one another. Do you suppose Jesus took Peter by the hands, looked into his brown eyes and said to him, 'Peter, do you love me?' Exactly, if you ask me. So I ask you, when was the last time you took someone by the hands, looked into his or her brown eyes and said, 'I love you?' He did not seem to mind. And he did speak to me.

Yes, I know we are pretty cool. Maybe even a little cold. For one thing, we would not want anyone to think we were gay, would we? I might say, though, that there is not much love even among gays. And so we keep it cool.

On the other hand, where are the norms we go by? Who is our leader, our model? Calvin Coolidge? Henry Ford? Are we based in Detroit or Nazareth, Massachusetts or Galilee?

We identify with cold blooded Anglo-Saxons and are happy with that, aware of course that Jesus was a southern type, olive skin and all from being in the sun. Those people were softer, warmer than we are. Were then, are now. In other words, if this dialogue had taken place on the shores of Lake Michigan and Jesus had been born in Indiana, the whole thing would have come off differently. I see, only I don't believe it. I think Jesus would be as warm in Maine as on the shores of the

Mediterranean. I think we are worldly. We take our measure not by Jesus but by someone like Ronald Reagan, a man's man. He does not, and we do not, go around asking others if you love me. And if we do, they do not reply. It is not done.

Why, we don't even have the words. Look how the translators struggle. Jesus called out to his disciples over the water and he used a term that somehow conveyed the extraordinary relationship between them and him. We do not have a word for that kind of love. We are inept and awkward in communicating his love. We fear it, for love is an enormous power. Hence we must restrain it. It's like a lot of sex. All through history people have tried to curb it, control it, keep it in hand, through law, custom, tradition, through modesty in thought, in word, in clothing. We fear sex unleashed and sometimes build such high walls around it that it almost disappears. Then another generation comes along and tears all the walls down. We live in such a tear-down age but we will soon begin building again.

But I do not see that we have to have such high walls around love. We should not have to be so modest about it that one wonders if it is even there. You read, surely, years ago in *Monastic Exchange* of what the old monks at the gate at Genesee Abbey wrote. Two big teaching orders of nuns and brothers had those fashionable, expensive self-studies made after Vatican II to find out what was wrong with them. Father said that it was really ironic. When the man came to each group at the end with his final report the scene was the same. If you want it in one sentence he said, 'Your people simply do not love one another'. Mostly I think it is because we are afraid to love. Hence the Easter greeting: Fear not!

I am not offering you cheaply what the dear brothers and sisters paid dearly for. I ask you only live with this morning's scene awhile and listen to what they are saying to one another.

If Jesus has great things in mind for us, and I believe he does, then he will want to be sure we love him. We will say so and say it again and again—that we love him I mean. And we will say it to our brothers in this boat with us, after this long night of no fish, as we sit down together with him to eat bread still hot and fish fresh from the sea and the fire. We will do that indeed on the eternal shores where he waits if we begin now. Then anyone could say even without a costly survey, 'Your people love one another'.

19

HIROSHIMA DAY ♣

Just as there is small point in a monk being a celibate unless he has a strong sense of the male's profound spiritual relationship to the feminine, so too there is not much use in becoming a monk without an experience of the strong bond every human has with every other human. It is this experience that faith builds on and to which it gives expression. It is entering this mystery with the response of love in Christ which is the basic work of the monk.

We deal with one aspect of this history today in remembering the history of some thirty years ago: the dropping of great bombs over two Japanese cities in August 1945. Humankind still endeavors to come to some understanding of what went on there and of the consequences. As Americans, we are involved, as human beings we are part of it, as members of the body of Christ we are deeply concerned. This is obvious. What is not so obvious is what we should do.

If prayer is a part of our life, so too is work, the manufacturing of fruit cake and cheese, their distribution and our consequent engagement in the economic life of our nation, its government and therefore its taxes, its foreign policies, its military forces. These are part of the scene of our lives, and however subtle the relation we have to these realities, the relation is undoubtedly there.

What is much harder to measure is our responsibility. We are likely to try to discount responsibility by reason of the trivial character of our involvement. Indeed, how valid is the claim that we are responsible for what goes on in this country?

When I was a child the two tallest buildings in the United States and maybe in the world were the Woolworth Building in New York and the Wrigley Building in Chicago, one built on profits of the five-and-ten-cent store and the other on profits of penny chewing gum. Some of that profit came from me. I maintain that our relationship to what goes on here in America is strictly that same penny and nickel-and-dime variety. The only thing wrong with that view is that millions of others with their pennies and nickels and dimes are what made skyscrapers possible and world wars and atom bombs part of history.

The gospel passage I just read [Luke 10:29–37: The Good Samaritan] has a suggestion to make to you. Let me suppose for a moment that the story that Jesus told becomes a dream, and that we interpret that dream. We would begin by asking, who is this person fallen among robbers? And who is this priest, this Levite? And who is the Samaritan? And who are the original robbers? I believe we would eventually get to the center of the dream and come to realize that in some way all of them are us. We are the center of the dream and appear in it in many ways. The one fallen by the way is ourselves. And we are the priest passing by, the Levite who had other things to do, the Samaritan who showed mercy. But, mind you, we are also the band of thugs and the innkeeper, too.

Our fellow Americans made the bomb and they dropped it. Our own military force carried out these operations. Doing this has been called an enormous evil. The victims thus are not only the Japanese of Hiroshima and Nagasaki, but also the citizens of the United States of America.

We beat the man up, left him dead, and we are the Levite passing by, the one too wise to get involved, who minds his own business and leaves bad enough alone. And we are the priest on his way to a function for the glory of God. Perhaps the priest was wondering what the man could have done to merit such treatment, for we get what we deserve, do we not? And we are also, let's face it, the no-account good Samaritan, the anti-hero bright people call stupid and rich people call poor. Beautiful people call such people trash, the least likely to succeed in the class who, surprisingly, come off winners. The bottom of the totem pole comes out on top, last in the pecking order and head of the lot. Probably the closest anyone in our society comes to the Samaritan is the gay. Not many, monks included, cotton to gays. If we are all the people in this dream, are now, or have been, or could be, it is as the Samaritan that we would be most uncomfortable. Had we been listening to Jesus tell this story, would we have considered a Samaritan the hero of the tale? Anyone around us would have considered him someone beneath contempt. Why, pray, do you think Jesus made him the hero?

But the dream, as all dreams do, leaves us with a choice. We can make it now or later or not at all. If we make a choice and a good one, the dream will never return. If we do not choose, or choose ill, the dream will return, Christ will try again.

The point is, I think, to forgive. Forgive me, dear brothers and sisters, for what I have done and your brothers and sisters for what they have done and yourself for what you have done. A total forgiveness includes everyone, everything. You can do that right here, right now. In fact that is what we are here for.

As robber, as Levite, as priest, forgive yourself. The victim forgives, for the victim is Christ. And the Samaritan forgives, for the Samaritan is Christ too. And the innkeeper is Christ. Christ is the center of this dream. He is at the heart of everyone in it, however hidden, however much betrayed. He is hidden in the brigands, too. You know that.

I am not talking fiction but realities. Truth. Grace. Pennies and nickels and dimes gathered together make a fortune and erect towers to prove the power of capitalism. Pennies and nickels and dimes build a kingdom of justice and peace and love, a kingdom a long time coming, but coming for all that. It is our penny forgiveness that hastens the coming. Otherwise, unforgiving, we go around and around, endlessly repeating evil on evil and worse each time round, generation after generation.

Wake up, sweet brother. And listen to your dreams.

20

THE GREY BEES 🐝

When, in August 1946, my mother asked me what I
wanted her to wear—what color, that is—for my
ordination and First Mass, I told her to wear grey.
And she did. What my mother had forgotten to reckon with
was my being color blind. To me, grey looks pink. So she wore
a pink tailored suit, and by happy circumstance—for my world
of color is my own—I got her a gladiolus from the garden to
give her as a corsage. It was, she told me, salmon pink and went
well with grey.

Grey, of course, is an integration of black and white. But
it is also associated with death. Years ago undertakers softened
black into grey hearses and coffins. When someone has an ashen
color we do not think that person a picture of health. Yet if we
combine grey with the color of fire and blood we end up with
something very challenging.

I am intrigued that your team is called the Grey Bees. It is
very beautiful. It perfectly suits the role you fill here in the
providence of God, for you are all perforce color blind. This is
not to say that you do not see colors, but you are blind to them
as signals of acceptance or rejection. You see color as the glory
of God, no matter where, and would never use it as a basis of
discrimination. All colors are beautiful. That you have in your
school a score of various peoples is indeed Pentecostal red and
that, in the grey of a disintegrating part of town, is something
to take joy in.

The fact that the bee is the symbol of your school is something
else again, for the bee finds honey even here, proving that you

find what you look for and believe in. There is honey hidden in your environment, in your people. You know it and you prove it, both the bees on the roof and the monks who work with them. The bee is not, as it were, robbing anyone of anything but providing what good there is if one would look for it, cultivate it, nurture it and share in it. Here where you live between a city quite splendid and a city no longer what it was, you have flowers and green and bees and, of course, the honey which is the point of it all. I mean love.

I think that this is what America is all about: integration, interaction, intermingling, so that a new spirit may be kindled and fresh stimulus given. When the Irish began to pour in hungry hordes into Boston, many years ago, the residents had long since established a lovely city—for the Yankees or the Anglo-Saxons or the WASPS, however you term them, had a highly developed civic sense and had made of Boston a significant city with handsome parks and public buildings and cultural centers, not to say residential areas of taste, green with trees and neat with pride. The Irish made a shambles of a lot of this. We were ignorant, brawling, and drunken. People regarded us as trash and I suppose in some ways we were. We were, after all, not running away from paradise when we came to these shores. It took time, but by doing dirty work, and by way of the priesthood and politics and the police and the fire departments, we slowly moved up and on and often out, to leave others to carry on with the same sorry, sad, and seemingly inevitable story: Italians and then Latinos, Hispanics, Blacks. In the process they contributed enormous good to the nation, as so many others have done and still do. They are not unique.

The grey bee finds honey where one would swear there was none. The monks back home in Gethsemani will think I am telling them tales when I refer to bees on the roof on Newark Abbey providing honey for the table of the monks, just as our bees do back of the house in the midst of a thousand acres of woods and pasture.

How very Benedictine that these men of peace should be peace, sow peace, and reap peace in this unlikely wilderness.

So your bees are not grey to me, that is to say, they are—you are—warm with the spirit in a gentle sort of way, quietly going about the business of finding good in all and drawing it forth from them to their good, to the good of all, to the glory of God. One could do worse. I doubt if we could do better. God bless the Grey Bees. May they find in the green that covers so much of the sprawl between gutted memories the golden sweetness no one ever thought was there. There was a time when only the wax they made was good enough for the lights on the altar. If we use something a little less symbolic, it is only because it has become more precious. Sweetness and light. Amen.

Note: Saint Benedict's Preparatory School at Newark Abbey in Newark, New Jersey, uses the grey bee as the school symbol. It began with the use of the letter B in grey (one of the school colors: the other is red) given in award at the year's end. This led a newspaper writer to refer to them as the Grey B's and thus the Grey Bees. Since the monks keep bees on the roof, it seemed to me a very good symbol.

21

Saint Columba, On Christmas Eve ♣

I t is told of Saint Columba, Irish monk of the sixth century, that when his end drew near all the monks of Iona grew sad. One of the monastery horses wandered into the enclosure where Columba was sitting in the sun and putting his head into the saint's lap, wept because he was soon to die. Columba praised God for this tenderness.

This legend may be the fruit of Celtic imagination, but I have taken it for real. For one thing, many saints, and monks in particular, have had a love for animals. For another, anyone who knows animals knows how uncanny is their intuition; how they can detect a person's fear, guess what is on one's mind, what a person wants to do. It is not impossible that they can recognize a heart of love. Columba was a man of love.

It seems to me, in contrast, that I am not a man without hate. This becomes clear in working even a little with horses these past months. How often have I been impatient, cruel, mean to them. They are basically gentle and submissive and only once in awhile are they contrary. They are only beasts, yet they have made me recognize what I have hidden from others and perhaps from myself.

This disturbs me. What if hate governs much of my life, is a factor behind much of what I do, a hidden constant. To be quite frank about it, there is the awful possibility that hatred had some part to play in my coming to the monastery. What I thought of as a kind of indifference to self and to the world, a contempt of comfort, pleasure, honor, privilege, a disdain of family, of travel—all of this may have been tinged with hatred without my realizing it.

So I think it would be good if monks could work with animals; cows and goats and pigs and sheep and horses and rabbits and even deer, if we had the chance. In working with them we could learn patience and love.

Yet the plan is not so simple, for we can very easily persist in hatred toward animals, in cruelty to God's creatures, and never be called to account for it. You can do things to animals you could not do to people.

Hate is something that lies deep within us. Only its expression is outside and then often disguised. When one hates one's work, for example, there may indeed be something wrong with the job, but it is more likely that there is something wrong with the person. Changing jobs merely changes the object of hatred.

Having entered the monastery, we learn the life and live it in a valid and generous way, and yet we may be enmeshed in hatred and not fully aware of it. In our relations with our superiors, our brothers, our work, the Rule, the regulations, customs—not to say in regard to our own person and to God—hatred may have a role. Actually, hatred is a major problem of our time. It is also a major problem of monks. Hatred is rampant in Mississippi, in the USA, in the Congo, and in my own heart.

Is this a gentle house? Is the first thing people think of when they come here that this is a place of love? The monks love one another? Has everyone who ever visited here sensed this? Has everyone who has ever been with this family for a longer or shorter time carried the perception that these are a kind folk, a gentle people? Do you yourself experience the monastery this way?

It could be that people think of it as a house of prayer, of penance, of work, of silence, of peace. And all of that is good and admirable. Regrettably, however, the first law is not a law of prayer or penance or work or silence or peace. It is love. This is the first law and the sum of the Law and the Prophets. 'By this shall all know that you are my disciples: that you love one another'.

Love, I admit, is a word that says everything and says nothing, for what is love to one is mush to another. Everyone has his or her own norms for love and has something specific in mind when wishing to be loved. In giving love one follows the light one has. Yet the gospels are not vague. The early Christians and the early monks were definite enough. They knew what love was: kindness, tolerance, not sitting in judgement, accepting wrong, suffering abuse, turning the other cheek, walking a second mile, giving a shirt when someone has taken your coat, laying down your life, not giving into wrath and anger; it is patience, endurance, bearing one another's burdens, not dominating or seeking to control others.

Everyone can see that these are the fruits of great love. They are not unknown among us. I believe this is a house of love, great love. I believe also that we always need to grow in love. We all see this need.

Is it not fascinating that people can span vast distances, cover oceans in hours, continents in moments, and talk about landing on the moon? In our own land people have built the largest bridges in the world, have suspended highways from wire across miles of water. Yet to cross the significant difference between one person and another, to cross the chasm between one heart and another, is another matter, another cup of tea.

When one monks' choir faces another, there is only one way to cross the gulf between them: by the song of love, by the voice of prayer. When I pray to the God who lies hidden in my brother and bow before him, I can reach the monk. Not otherwise. The most beautiful expression of fraternal love is the vision of peace when monks line up across from one another, not for conflict, not for strife, not to oppose one another, not to dominate or prevail over one another or bring influence to bear, but for the common praise of God Almighty's love. Until I can recognize this divine presence in people, love is impossible. It is impossible because I can see nothing there but the same ignorance, weakness and evil that is in myself and which I find loathsome. If I loathe what I am, I cannot love another. If I hate myself, I cannot love anyone.

And yet how can one come to love oneself when one feels unlovable? One can do so in the love that Christ has for every single person. If Christ loves me then I am lovable, no matter what I am. I can embrace and accept another, for that person too is loved no matter how wretched. For this is love: to accept the total reality of another person: weakness, failure, stupidity, and sins. It is to love not because the person is good—for who is good?—but to love in Christ's love.

This is why it is a scandal when only the good in a monastery are loved, but the weak are not: when people are loved for being efficient, or handsome, or generous, or virtuous, or regular. But when someone is inefficient, clumsy, rough, or mean, frail or laden with weakness, that person is not loved but harassed, chastened, reproved, castigated, relegated. Then the pious turn their piety on him to bring him into line. This is to love as pagans love. It is not Christian. If I want to know how much real love there is in a family, I ask the weakest member.

We make excuses of reasonableness, sweet reasonableness. Reason has nothing to do with it. There is nothing reasonable about Christ's love for us. It is beyond reason, beyond human reckoning, beyond human fathoming. Pagan love is reasonable; Christ's love is not. It is unreasonable. It is ridiculous, it is foolish, it is madness. And I can prove it. First proof: Christ loves me. Second proof: he loves you. Third proof: we love each other.

This kind of love is a divine gift. It is not purchased, or merited, or bought. Nor is it simply a matter of good breeding or good manners, as if Christianity were a means to a charming personality, something anyone can attain to with a little good will, effort and concentration. It is simply beyond human capacity. It is a gift. We must ask for it, repeatedly, without ceasing. And the intensity of our asking will be consequent to our awareness of the need. How profoundly we recognize our need to love and be loved.

I think we have a greater need than anyone else in the world. I do not think there are any people anywhere poorer than we are. If Christ gives his love where it is needed, he will give it here, for here is the greatest need. Into the chaos of our own hearts he must pour the abundance of his love. He must root out forever all power of hate, tear out any hideous madness by which we turn on one another. He must come into our darkness with his light, into our cold and chilled chambers with his love, into our barren halls with his kindly love.

There is no place in Kentucky, no place in America, no place in the world, where the need can be any greater, for we live with our poverty and face it inexorably, stripped of all delusions, barren of pretense and vanity, open to the winds of the spirit that drive away all the fogs that might hide our rags. We live with ourselves and with each other. We know both.

If there is need and the need is admitted, he will come. 'Come then, Lord Jesus. We cannot live without love. You descended into the darkness of your mother's womb, you were hidden in the womb of the earth and from the dark cave came forth into the world. You hid again in the earth in the grotto of the garden of Gethsemani and sweat blood in anguish over sin and death. You descended again into the womb of the earth and lay there three days dead in the tomb. O God of light, descend into the darkness of our depths. Come, be present in the womb of our time. Come, be present in space on earth our mother. Come, suffer in us the anguish of our birth, the coming of the great day. All the world, the whole universe, is heavy with expectancy; the time of delivery is at hand. We groan for the fulfillment of all things. In this darkness be present, in this agony be with us, lest we perish.'

In this long and mysterious death we press toward a long and unknown future, toward a life for which we know no dimensions. All of humankind is being swept forward in this movement to eternity. This cosmic birth, this universal gestation, is the great work we all are engaged in, the great redemptive fulfillment in Christ. In this darkness we fear, and it is fear that leads us to hate. As frightened as animals we turn on one another. We are afraid of the dark, of the unknown. Being afraid, we hate; hate the darkness, hate ourselves, hate others. Seeking to escape from reality, we act in fear to preserve the reality we have. We are people in a dark cave gathering around a flickering fire, frightened by the shadows in the walls, the grotesque figures and eerie shapes, and we blame others for them. Into this cosmic cave Christ has come; into this darkness light is born. He tells us there is nothing to fear.

We are afraid of losing our small hold on reality. We occupy so small a space, have so fragile a grasp on existence, that every expression of our significance is vitally important. What I say, what I think, what I have, what I want, what I am used to, what I do, are part of me, are me. When you do not take me seriously, when you offend me, abuse me, oppose me, when you are superior to me, or are indifferent to me, you make my existence nothing. Therefore I fear you, and fearing come to hate you. I hide it, of course, but from a horse I need not hide when he makes me look ridiculous by being indifferent to my commands. This horse, who is quite capable of killing me in a matter of seconds, I can abuse.

What is the answer to this, except to say that all the reality we take hold of to assert our significance will be taken away? The space we stand in, the words we say, the deeds we do, our thoughts, our desires—all will be taken. And what will be left? Only love and what springs from love. Love will be all that we have because love is all that we are. A person is created in love; love is the only real world we live in. Love is the only reality. We, each of us, were conceived in a moment of human love, but in that moment lay hidden an act of divine love so exquisite that no tongue can speak of it. All earthly love together is but a stumbling semblance of it.

This vision of reality is had only from Christ. In this vision is the end of fear, and if the end of fear, the end of hate. Alive in the world of love, we can put our arms down, can relax tight fists, can open hand and heart, and in the darkness with others await the great day which is to come, the day close at hand. A bird of passage can pass through this life of many births and many deaths, taking nothing with it but love. It is made possible by Christ. He has given point to our lot. He has entered into life, into death, into suffering, pain, darkness. He has given them all meaning, made them holy. All birth and all death is now sacred. Suffering and pain are touched with the divine. The darkness may be darkness still, but it is filled with the light of God. And we have no need to fear, we have only to love one another.

'Fear not,' the angel said, 'for behold I bring you good tidings of a great joy that shall be to all people. For this day is born to you a savior who is Christ the Lord, in the city of David. And this shall be a sign unto you. You shall find the infant wrapped in swaddling clothes and laid in a manger.'

It is appropriate that the word should have been given to shepherds keeping watch over the sheep, just as it was appropriate that in the cave where the Lord was born were more animals present than humans, animals who knew they were in the presence of a great love. Dear God, that we might know this night that we are forever in the presence of a great love.

It is Christmas Eve and it is the time for wishes, so I am going to make a wish. I wish God would send us a saint. And soon. The saint need not be anything special. God has been good to us, very good. We are provided for. Our needs are met. But we need a saint.

We need someone who believes in love, who believes God loves this place, believes God loves me, believes God loves everyone, and believes this strongly, intensely—so strongly and intensely that its great power releases great powers of love—in so great a reality that the fire of hate languishes and dies.

Let this person take a place in the community. Let this saint do what God wants. Let this person have faults and shortcomings and fail and be wrong sometimes. Let this person share as deeply as possible in our common concerns, our endeavors, our struggles and dreams. But let the saint believe in love.

For this is holiness. This is sanctity: to believe in the love of God—to believe God loves this house and everyone in it. To believe God loves this world and everyone on it.

Tonight in the cave of Bethlehem, God loves. We have only to say Amen to it again and again, today and everyday as long as we live.

22

Hatred of God ✤

We hear a lot about the love of God—at least in religious circles—but we do not hear a great deal about the hatred of God. I think it might be good to say something about it lest the impression be given that there is no such thing or that it is not something to reckon with in the life of the spirit. I mean, of course, hatred of God not in others, but in ourselves, in our own hearts.

Hatred of God in other people is fairly easy to see. I do not primarily mean the obvious hatred expressed in crushing and curbing religion, destroying churches, suppressing schools or the religious press or freedom of religious assembly. All this is common enough, even in our own times. I refer instead to the more subtle, but no less genuine, hatred of God which operates in the world of religion itself, within the Christian faith. Christ, as anyone who can read the Gospels knows well enough, made specific references to this great agent of human behavior. People do strange things 'for the love of God'. He knew what he was talking about. His own death was an instance of it.

There is no nation in Catholic Europe, I would suggest, that at sometime or other has not turned with unbridled hatred on the Catholic faith that was its heritage—one can mention Italy or France or Portugal or Spain. During and after the Reformation, it is clear enough, Christian hatred for Christian took on a whole new dimension. Ruined cathedrals and abbeys are as common in Europe as statues with the heads lopped off. History is full of hideous strife rooted in religion. Nor is it unknown today.

What we are prone to overlook in all this is the hidden truth: that there is a hatred of God in the human heart that wants out. God is a spirit and so hatred of him is a problem. We humans consist of matter as well as spirit. Any hatred of God, then, is necessarily going to be manifested in a human way, involving body as well as soul. We cannot destroy God, but we can destroy churches. We cannot hate God, but we can hate priests.

In Catholic times, history reveals to us, conflict was no rarity. Even within specifically religious groups, animosities and tensions frequently arose between religious orders. Though for centuries Jews lived in peace among Catholic peoples, there were times when hatred for them would flare up and manifest itself in gross cruelty. There never has been an era in which some heresy or other did not declare itself; and attitudes towards heretics some times and in some places, certainly not always, were not merely hostile, but vindictive and punitive. A whole age displayed a violence toward witches that seems to us to have been hysterical and mad. All these phenomena, and they run all through our religious history, are expressions of hatred for God, though all those involved would insist that hatred of God had nothing to do with it. It was all done for the love of God.

That people could do such things for the love of God seems repulsive to someone not involved, to one viewing it from a distance in time and space. And yet, a little understanding of the human heart suggests that love is a very ambivalent business with us. Contemporary wife-beating is almost epidemic, yet many of these wives are dearly loved by their husbands. Child abuse has become so rife in the USA that the Catholic bishops devoted serious study to it and published their study for dissemination to all the faithful. It does not follow that abused children are not loved, though this is often the case. It is never a matter of hatred being mixed with love that is the mystery.

Oscar Wilde in 'The Ballad of Reading Gaol' has the line, 'yet each man kills the thing he loves'. There is profound truth in his insight. Hatred with us humans is often the other face of love.

In the Catholic tradition, the Eucharist has never been seen as only a memorial meal, a supper of communion with Jesus around a common table. It has been that, but the Church has also insisted that the Mass is also a sacrifice, that it not only commemorates but also reenacts Christ's death on the cross. It is a sacrifice offered by a priest standing at an altar. We are confronted with a truth: Jesus was put to death. And we, we humans, are the ones who did it, out of hatred for God.

The traditional Christian symbol is the cross, but Catholic usage has favored not the simple cross, but the cross with the image of Christ's body on it in death. This vivid reminder is always before us, the Son of God as a human being nailed to the tree by us.

Though this may well be on an unconscious level, below the surface as it were, the impact of Calvary is profound in that it forces us to confront the reality of the hatred in our hearts. In other words, there are strange areas of darkness within us. Unless these dark areas are acknowledged, confronted, resolved, we are always in grave danger that they will, all of a sudden, take on power and emerge in behavior that we ourselves will be the last to understand. Worse, we may permit such forces to emerge willingly, consider them expression of the love we are certain fills our breasts.

Those who count on the innocence and goodness of the human heart are unconscionably naive. None of us would maintain that we are depraved and wholly corrupt, but to deny that there are strange aspects of human behavior is to be blind. It is clear enough from simply reading the papers that people do indeed do dreadful things, and the emergence of widespread violence in our time fills most people with enormous anxiety and fear. No small part of this reaction stems from the most frightening realization of all, that there is within my own heart some reservoir which might erupt into the very same violent activity which I so roundly condemn in others. In fact, the intensity of my condemnation in part reassures me that I could not, would not, will not allow anything of the sort to come out of me.

Tight control notwithstanding, strange things may come out all the same, and come out as love. At least we call it love, indeed, insist it is love. When you are walking with someone else through the bush or on some tricky ground and you slip or trip, your companion will be very quick to say, 'Oh, sorry,' and let you think that in some way he is responsible. Once is all right, but when this is repeated time and again, it annoys.

In the world of politics, nations, races, all this is strong enough. Good Christian people are easily reconciled to hating others who are of a different nation, a different race. With a different religion the situation is even worse. The ethnic conflict of the Gael and the Gaul through the centuries is nothing to the hatred between Catholic and Protestant and that in turn is mild in comparison to the hatred between Christian and Moslem.

Key words are often a give-away. For some Protestants, words like Vatican, pope, bishop, priest, hierarchy, Rome, Jesuit, are enough to call up a whole galaxy of emotional reactions, all extremely negative. The same can be said of Catholics in reference to Protestants, not to say Jews, Arabs, Moslems and others. Any gay person can wax eloquent in describing the unspeakable loathing people have for him—these good Christian folk.

Yet, in a tolerant ecumenical climate we have made great progress in overcoming the animosity we inherited toward those who differ from us. This is a blessing. Yet I am not sure the overall picture has much changed. The ground may have shifted, but the action is the same. I gather we really need something to hate, something to look down on, something to loathe, something to be the object of our violence.

I do not see how any progress at all can be made until we see how hate stems from a basic hatred for God. We sense that God does not love us, for obvious reasons, and so we respond by not loving God, by hating God. And since we cannot hate God who is pure spirit, we hate whatever is capable of receiving that hate, the Church or any of God's creatures. I do not see how we can move one inch further along the road to love and the abandonment of hatred until we acknowledge the presence of this hatred for God in us.

We hate God for what we are and for what we are not, for what we have or do not have, for what God has done or for what God has not done. All this hate makes a dark pool deep down inside us, far below the surface of our day to day conscious existence, but there, very much there. It is this hatred which is the fount of all the expressions of contempt and loathing that come out of us in thought, in word, in deed. The ugly word, the fist, the gun, the look, the feeling, all express something so hidden we are not aware of it. And all such expressions we invariably justify. We had good reason to think, to say, to do what we did. In fact, we did it out of love. And if you push the matter, did it out of love for God. Unacknowledged hatred comes out identified as love. Often enough we end up hating what we love and do not know it. We do not know it because we do not want to know. We are capable of the most monstrous actions which we identify as love.

The mystery of Christ on the cross and its continuance among us in the Eucharist is the key. Once we see Calvary as the fruit of hatred and the expression of God's love, we can reconcile the terrifying vision of our own reality. By pondering the cross and by entering into its depth we can slowly be reconciled to our own reality, break the power of hatred, soften it, diminish it, and finally banish it from our hearts by the power of God's love for us.

Unless and until that is done we will be forever split on the love-hatred dilemma and will identify all we do as love at work. Well-meaning Christians can be literally filled with hatred—hatred for self, hatred for others—and not be at all aware that the basic hatred gnawing at them is a hatred for the God they love.

If we did not hate God, we would never have crucified the Son. But our faith tells us that we did just that. Now we look on what we have done, see the fruit of hate, and see it by the power of God changed into a mystery of love. It is through hatred we come to love. That does not mean that hatred is a way toward love, or that hatred leads to love or is a school of love. It means rather that only in a total awareness of what we are can we come into a total experience of God. Any awareness of what we are means awareness that the reverse side of human love is hatred. The heart we love God with is a new heart, given us by God, a heart of total love, purged of hatred made wholly divine.

23

BROTHER MAURUS' JUBILEE ❧

In one of Sigrid Undset's novels a story is told by the priest on the medieval manor of Kristin. A young servant was accused of stealing a silver ring. This servant, a character of exceptional sensitivity and nobility, was so shocked by the false charge that she could not endure it. She went off to the lake nearby, intending to drown herself for very shame and outrage. She walked into the lake and felt within her a great warmth and upsurge of feeling, noted how welcome the waters felt, how lovely was the landscape around, the sky above. She did indeed experience a sort of exaltation of spirit as she went to her death. And then, somehow inspired, she made the sign of the cross and called on the name of Jesus. Instantly the feelings of fervor disappeared, the lake felt cold, the milieu seemed drab and grey, the whole context barren of spiritual tone. At once she realized how stupidly she was acting, how much in the evil spirit, and she came out of the lake and forgot her intentions. Later, all was cleared up and she was restored to peace and honor.

Doing hard things, putting yourself to death, is common enough. It happens all the time. People put themselves to great trouble, undergo great trials, in order to achieve something they think worthwhile. They not only expose themselves to death, but actually put themselves to death if they think something may be achieved by it. Just look at the Guiness *Book of World Records* if you want to learn what some people are willing to do to get a bit of glory, to have some sort of name, at least some significance in the world scene. The pursuit of money, fame, and power are goals pursued with enormous ambition. Professional people seek eminence in their special fields with a drive that is literally consuming. Father Louis told me that many professional people burn with jealousy and envy, a result of the total commitment to their specialty.

It is the name of Jesus and the sign of the cross that will give us the light of truth, that will cast over the false glamour of human ambition and pride a realism which exposes them for what they are. In the light of eternity a great deal of human assertion looks tawdry and trifling, and is.

We have gathered in this chapel to give thanks to God for the grace given a man who also chose spiritual death, who also set out to achieve something, who also dedicated himself to the pursuit of a goal that involved him in much trouble, trial and suffering. And happily, when we invoke the name of Jesus and when we make the sign of the cross, the light then given does not expose what this man has done as something petty and inconsequential, shot through with human pride and arrogance, but fifty years in the service of God of a special kind, a service marked by the secret, the hidden, the humble and little.

To say more than that would I think border on the irreverent and the crude.

But we can rejoice with our brother, with his family, his kin and with one another this day. For God is good and that goodness is manifest here. And if Jesus asks much and has not many friends because he does ask much, let us thank God for the good friends he does have and rejoice in them.

It is a great tragedy for a person to learn, as so many people eventually do, that the dream to which they have given themselves with so much ardor and zeal has been a delusion, a fantasy. How great the joy, on the other hand, to find, as so many do, that the dream they gave themselves to in Jesus turns out to be so much more than they could possibly have imagined, that they are shamed for not having done more, tried harder, lived and loved more earnestly. For the light of God's truth sheds its warm glow over all the human scene for the eyes of faith, and makes clear that to little ones has been revealed the secrets of the kingdom of heaven. God bless you, brother Maurus, now and in the kingdom. God bless the day so long ago when you turned your steps to Gethsemani. You could not have known then what a journey you were setting out on. Nor can you know now the ultimate result of it all. But this much we do know and rejoice in: that they are blessed who say goodbye and never look back, who give all away, who die gladly for the Lord. Amen.

24

ASCENSION ❧

I f you truly think of this place as Gethsemani, then, of
course, it is no problem for you to realize that Jesus ascended into heaven from a mount no further away, no
higher probably, than one of the knobs here in our woods to
the west. Indeed, if this is not true for you—that Jesus suffered
here, died, rose, and ascended from the Vineyard Knob, as it
were, in our very midst—then is this Christian story true for
you at all? Our salvation is not a matter of geography, place, or
chronology, time. It is here and now.

In this time after the ascension we are living in a sort of
suspended expectation, aware somehow that wonderful things
have taken place and that we have been witness to them, but
aware too, that something every bit as wonderful is about to
happen. The only stance in such a situation is prayer. Hence
we are at prayer these days and full of wondering.

While you are at it, I would suggest a diversion for you.
People at prayer need now and then some little something
to divert them, but not too much, just enough to assist their
attention.

Take twelve blank cards the size of an ordinary playing card,
and put six of them over here to your right and six of them over
here to your left. Take up one set of six and write the names
of six people that you know and like very much. I do not say
love, for we should love everyone, but six people whom you
like, you admire, you are taken with. It may be hard to limit
yourself to six, being the sort of people we are, but try to do
so. Put that six aside and take the other six and write on them

the names of six people you do not like. I do not say do not love—because we love all—but do not like: their temperament, their style, their way. I do not refer to sin. No one can like sin. I mean their disposition, their manner. Whatever. Again, you may have a hard time finding six you do not like, but be a bit fussy and sensitive for once and may be you can come up with six. Turn the cards over then one by one and write just a couple of words about what it is you like or do not like about each person. Then put the cards away until Pentecost.

The lesson we are to learn from the mystery we are to celebrate these days, the ascended Christ and the coming of the Spirit, is that Christ, Christianity, life and love and the kingdom, are not 'up there'. The angels say to the disciples, 'What are you standing here for looking up into heaven? He will be back, but he may be a long while coming.' The apostles did all there was to do. They went back to the city to await the Spirit who would teach them, touch them, with that fire which for so long has been burning in human hearts and burns there in human hearts all around you.

It is the Spirit who makes it possible for us to step out of time and so extend the horizons of our earth that we live in an eternal kingdom.

It is by the power of the Spirit that we live in that larger world that we were meant to live in, no longer blind and deaf, out of touch, unaware: no longer within the shell of an ego, the confines of a womb, under the ice of a frozen lake.

In the power of the Spirit we can cross the chasm that separates me from you, you from others, from the people across the table, across the aisle, across the street, the county, the country, the world. Infinite is the distance from one person to another, compassed only in the Spirit.

And because we are at this infinite distance, we are out of relation to ourselves also, we of infinite depth. It is the Spirit again who makes it possible for us to recognize our own truth, know our own reality, and thus have the freedom of the children of God. The joy of being truly myself, truly unique, is repeated in my joy, in your unique reality, that experience of Pentecost in which a multitude of many languages, of many lands, all heard the wonders of God in their own identity, a unique experience of common marvel.

On Pentecost, then, take your dozen cards, place them with the names down and read the brief legends on the back. You know whose description you read, whose character is delineated, if not perfectly, certainly in such terms that a little touch here and there would make it truly lifelike.

Here is the lesson Christ's spirit enkindles within us: that the least of my brethren is also me, as is the best of them. If I do not embrace them I am never at peace with myself, of which self they are, so many of them in so many ways mirrors of me.

The glorious experience of the Pentecost present and to come is this insight that all are one in Christ, the good and the bad of us, the dowered and the undowered, people from the least of cities or the most glamorous: the Medes and the Parthians and the Elamities and those from Mesopotamia and from Libya and beyond the Jordan; from Lebanon and Paducah, Cincinnati and Boston, Cleveland, Philadelphia, Wichita, Houston, Toronto, and Melbourne: English and Irish, Italian and Indian, Slav, Poles, African, German and French . . . all of us have heard in our own tongue, in the landscape of our own history, in the light and the shadow of our own character and temperament, the magnificent *mirabilia dei*, the marvelous works of God. Reason enough to be glad.

Throw your cards away. They are useless. Silly. Irrelevant. They are not true anymore. How can you talk of like and dislike for people loved of God? Can you say you do not like the sun, the moon, the Pacific Ocean? Can one not like the daisies in the meadow, now like the indigo bunting I saw yesterday in the bottoms, the rain pushy and aggressive? In the Spirit we can not only love ourselves, but like ourselves, something else again. We can love one another and even like one another. Love God and like Christ, in the Spirit. Now. And here. Amen.

25

STILL MAKING THE SUN SHINE AND THE MOON RISE ❧

Along time ago in a monastery north of us a young monk, dissatisfied and unhappy, realized that he was not going to get anywhere as a monk and left. It happens sometimes. As he went out the front gate he noticed Brother Anthony cutting the grass and he good naturedly waved good-bye to him and said, 'God bless, Brother Anthony. See you.' So the young man went back to school and got himself a degree, and being bright and gifted, found a very good job and a very lovely wife and in time came children and a nice home to go with them. Ten years ago he was vacationing in the Finger Lakes and thought he would stop by and say hello to the abbey of his youth, which he did. He left the family in the car and went across the yard. There was a monk cutting grass as before. And would you believe, it was Brother Anthony. 'God bless us, Brother Anthony, you still cutting grass?' Equal to the occasion Brother Anthony said cheerfully 'Yes. And still making the sun shine and still making the moon rise.'

A couple of years ago I was asked to give a retreat to a group of Lutheran missionaries. The request being a little unusual, given a background of traditional Lutheran-Catholic animosity there, it seemed appropriate to agree to accept. So I did. The time came when I had to get something ready for the Lutherans, and the closer it came the more distressed I became. What am I going to tell them? I know nothing about Lutheranism and nothing about ecumenism. I cannot give them a dated summary of Catholic teaching.

In the end I did what I always have done. I simply shared what was going on in my own heart. And I told them as much, using some of the talks I had earlier given to the fathers and brothers and sisters on the coast when I had been asked now and then to give a day of recollection or some reflections at a quarterly conference. I even used some of the chapter talks I had given here at Gethsemani, a batch of them having been sent me by a friend with whom I had left my papers. I was not long into this when first one, then another of the Lutherans came to me and said, 'Father, what you are giving us is just what we wanted. Just what we needed.' Fine. Good to hear that. They asked, 'Were you briefed on us beforehand? You seem right on target.' 'No,' I said, 'I was not briefed. I came green.' 'Well,' one of them said, 'we are in sore straits. Maybe you know of the theological turmoil in the Missouri Synod after the upheaval at the major seminary?' I said that I heard tell of it. 'What you do not know,' he said, 'is how all this has grievously affected our work here in the highlands: our finances and many of our projects had to be curtailed or dropped, not to mention the personal problems resulting from it all. Then you come and what you say is singularly fitting and helpful.'

So I told them later, at the end, 'Do you know what has happened to us these past days? The things I have shared with you are problems, difficulties, questions, I have worked with, have shared with my brothers and sisters on the coast, my brothers in the monastery, problems and questions they too cope with, contend with. Do you see how like one human heart is to another human heart? And how common are doubt and fear and worry and distress? How many followers of Christ face insecurity and loneliness, failure, misunderstanding? How we must deal with those frightening monsters of hatred and anger and despair that swim around in our depths and show themselves close to the surface now and then? There is no answer to any of this except in Christ. We meet in the heart and then and there discover that we are brothers and sisters in Christ.

What missionaries on the coast cope with, the monks back at the abbey, and the Missouri Synod Lutherans in the highlands of Papua, New Guinea, are at bottom remarkably similar. It appears, does it not, that ecumenism is a matter mostly of the heart, and of the experience of love.

In Christ, the monk, like anyone else, discovers sooner or later that it is not what he does that matters. Achievement, competence, talent, administration, leadership, endeavor, are all excellent human values we simply cannot live without. But of themselves they are not enough, even though we may be most of a lifetime discovering they are not. A monk cutting grass is significant in the scheme of things, not for the mowing but for the loving.

Christ is the salvation of the world, and significance comes from union with him. I would point out to you that this union is real. Without love Christ is not in this world. Without our love the sun does not rise, the moon does not shine in the night. When there is no response to Christ in the world, then Christ is not here. Without Christ the world collapses, disappears, disintegrates into nothingness, not worth a candle.

Only in the human can the divinity live and only in humankind is the humanity of Christ Jesus present. Only in human entrance into the mystery of Christ's birth and life, passion, death and resurrection, through the sacrament of human life in the love of God, is the world kept going and the redemption accomplished. Our significance then never lies in what we do or even who we are, but only in our love, and that love is pure gift, responded to, accepted, integrated.

Once the whole world was like a monastery, a place in which communion with God was easy. Primitive cultures are far more advanced than we are, without the civilization of frenzied noise and flurry, passion and violence, sometimes beautiful and often sophisticated but always drowning out the possibility for awareness, for pondering. Fewer and fewer places of refuge exist where, in quiet, reality can be heard, havens of the presence which gives the heart scope and the world its meaning. It is this commerce with the heart of God and with every human heart we touch that is most superbly significant in human existence. Ten years from now I may drop in at Genesee Abbey and see Brother Anthony or his equivalent cutting the grass, and happy at it. The sun rises because of him and the moon rises in our night. You would be surprised how many Anthonys there are. And not all of them are in monasteries. Some of them are Lutherans.

That is why they ask a man who wants to enter, 'Can you sing?' They do not necessarily mean, have you a good voice, can you read music? God be praised when it is so, but rather we should ask, 'Do you know what it means to sing the praise of God? Do you know how to make love? Otherwise not much point in coming here. It's no place to make something of yourself.' We make everything of Christ. He is our only significance. Amen.

26

Enlightened by a Gentle God ♣

You look at Salvador Dali's splendid study of the Last Supper and you wonder why all their heads are down, all twelve of them. Why do they not look up? What are they afraid of? See that grand room with its massive frame to guard all beneath, and yet open to glorious light, to the sweep of glassy waters and rugged mountains, and presiding at that handsome table a worshipful Christ, a beautiful Christ of glory. What are they frightened of? Why do they hide their faces, not daring to look?

Carl Gustav Jung came from a line of eminent Lutheran divines, yet he knew at root that he was, like most Europeans, Catholic. The thought of Rome haunted him and he knew that one day he would have to visit the city and accept its significance. It was years before he could bring himself to do so and even then he got no further than the ticket seller's window. There, just before he asked for a ticket to Rome, he fainted. He concluded that he was simply not equal to it and never went.

Thomas Merton, before his baptism, dropped in at Saint Bonaventure's College with his friend Robert Lax. He was no sooner there than he demanded in angry terms that Lax drive him out of the place. 'Let's get out of here.' He meant what he said and they left. 'The elemental fear of the citizen of Hell,' he wrote of it.

Peter, James, John on Mount Tabor fell asleep. It was not that they were weary. It was just too much reality, that's all. More that they could cope with.

The disciples in the garden fell asleep. Again, it was not that they were tired. They were frightened beyond words, beyond consciousness.

Our Cistercian abbots gathered at Conyers Abbey to discuss what was taking place at this and that community. The new constitutions were read and 'well received', or 'well accepted by all' or 'made a good impression'. These statements come not from a poll or survey, but are simply on-the-spot reactions to a group message, not necessarily spoken but certainly experienced.

Because we give off vibrations we send out messages. These impulses can radiate love or contempt or anger. No matter how plausible our face, how pleasant our toothy smile, the vibrations will send out our real message. A face as unlikely as Mother Teresa's can transmit enormous love, and a very lovely face can transmit loathing. Children are almost infallible in seeing into people. Primitives too. And monks.

The major dialogue is the silent one. This place, this house, sends out powerful streams of God, for God is very much here. Palpably.

But if people can fall asleep when Christ is in glory on Tabor, if people can fall asleep when Christ is in his poignant hour of grief in the Garden of Olives, and if at the Supper Dali portrays the likes of us hiding our faces, then, what of now?

Did Ambrose Southey[1] catch something when he wrote us that 'there was a certain amount of apathy in our service of God'.

Primitives like to stand in the fear of the Church, they like to line the walls. Even machos are timid, you know. That is why they are macho.

These then are the reasons he comes in bread and wine.
    Lest he frighten us.
And why he stoops to wash our feet.
    Lest we shy away in fear.
God is a gentle God.

1. Abbot General of the Cistercian Order, Strict Observance, 1973–1990.

God is a kindly God.
And God for all that.
And yet we are so frightened by that Presence
   so threatened,
   so aroused,
   so angered, so overwhelmed with anger,
   that we kill it.
Figure that out.

It may take you an eternity to do so. Meanwhile what you have figured out so far is the message you give out all day long, every day. It is your witness, the sermon you preach. It is your response to Tabor, your Gethsemani, your upper room where Jesus washes your feet and serves you a supper you will never forget. Amen.

27

PAIN AND THE LOVE OF GOD ♣

One of the dark secrets of life that I have been a long time learning is that love is rarely acceptable to us humans save in relation to pain. I do not know that I have it clear in my own mind yet exactly why this is, but that it is so seems to me unassailable.

The relationship between pain and love is very deep, that is sure. Who knows love knows pain. Pain is often an expression of love.

This past week in the refectory we heard in the reading from Robert Massie's *Peter the Great* the awesome story of a long-tortured victim who under severest suffering did not and would not break down and confess. Yet he literally collapsed into the Tsar's arms and revealed his whole story when that leader turned to kindness and lavished love, kisses, embraces, and bright promises. What leather whips and burning brands could not do, tenderness did. And, alas, I could not help thinking that the man would never have believed in the Tsar's love, would never have been able to receive it, had he not first known pain. It was pain that made it possible for him to accept that remarkable love. And do you know, the love of God will mean nothing to us until we know what pain is. A dreadful thing to say, but I fear it is true.

Jesus tells us as much this morning in the gospel reading, when he says, 'Unless you take up your cross and follow me you cannot be my disciple', a saying which, in our fashion, we customarily misunderstand. We think Christ means some cross of our own making, sacrifices and penances and good works and what not, all done for him. No, dear friends. The little tokens you and I offer to God are nothing at all when we look at things honestly. Is it not cruel enough that life must end, that we must part from everyone we have known and loved, that every bit of loveliness and beauty that has been ours must be given away? Jesus tells us how stupid it is to gather up wealth. You cannot take it with you, poor fool. You will die as naked and as penniless as you were born.

Life comes to us, too, by way of pain. Pain is our common language. Everyone speaks this tongue. It is a universal experience. We love it. We are so used to it that we cannot do without it. It is the only way we feel right, feel comfortable. When we do not have it we create it. Jesus broke the power of this fanatic addiction, this absurdity, by taking pain on himself. His entrance into pain and death spelled the end of both. There is no power left in them, not any more.

So Jesus, looking on us, knowing our ways, seeing our lot, recognizing our plight, simply turns the whole thing inside out. It is through pain that you will become not merely my disciples, not merely my friends, but one with me— forever.

The pain is there anyway, anyhow. Life, no matter how long, is short, an exercise in futility for many. Even for the elegant and beautiful it is something that will end in rot and decay. In the face of all that we have the glorious message of Christ that through his human descent into pain and death we will enter into life. There is meaning, there is a point, there is a purpose. There is salvation, freely given, had for nothing. And, of course, not accepted. Who can believe it?

But the secret is out. It is through suffering that we are able to accept, to receive. Faith becomes real to us through pain. Jesus called it the cross. It is there anyway and has been all along, but it is by faith that it comes alive.

As monks you and I are not called upon to develop elaborate techniques in pain and suffering. There is more than enough of that already. We have to do something much more arduous: enter into the human heart and not hate it, not destroy it, not wound it, but love it as Jesus does. In loving that one heart, love every heart alive, all in the heart of the Lord of love whose heart is the heart of the universe.

28

A Playful Greeting ♣

Once, in time past, when I lived on a hill by the sea, it was the wont of the bishop of the area to swoop down and greet me whenever he flew up the coast. To be sure, this was no great thing, yet it did involve some response on my part, for if he flew low, in his Cessna, that meant I did not hear it until it got fairly close, leaving me the very little time to get out of the house to the grass out front so that I could wave to him as he swept low and dipped his wings to me. It became a sort of play between us, a little game we indulged in once in a while. I used to think about it, wondering why the man bothered. Just a little change in a two-hundred mile flight? A bit of a whimsy? A little nonsense for the fun of it? He was no boy, was a bishop almost as long as I have been a priest. Nor was he, is he, the lighthearted, happy go lucky sort, but a long gaunt, Iowa farmer of solid German stock, now as brown and withered from the sun as his native corn late in the season.

Let me tell a story of the same man. A young man had just finished seminary college and wondering about the next step and, not sure, thought he might like to serve three years in the South Pacific as a lay missionary. So the general manager of the mission made some inquiries about him and got a not very enthusiastic report. In fact, the returning letter spoke in disparaging terms and did not recommend that the young man's offer be accepted. So the manager went to the bishop, letter in hand, to see what the bishop would do. 'The report on him is no good,' the bishop heard him say, and he took the letter and said to his assistant, 'Does this young man really want to come?'

'Yes. No doubt about that, he wants to come.'

'Well then,' said the bishop, 'tell him to come.' With that he dropped the letter into the waste basket without taking a look at it. The young man did come and he did very well. For the bishop, you see, had enough experience with volunteers, if not with human nature in general, to know that reports and opinions and recommendations or the lack of them have only a relative value, sometimes a very relative value. Time had shown that a South Sea experience was not something with predictable results. The most highly recommended candidate might turn out to be a disaster, the less well spoken of might do very well. The bishop knew that and was not too timid to act on it.

With these two items I have described a man in whom the spirit of youth was very much alive. And it is on this that I would like to dwell a few moments, and that thought I would like to leave with you on the feast of Saint Benedict. If there is one very definite impression that I get, it is this: we do not think of Saint Benedict as youthful. In fact, I am weary beyond telling of hearing him depicted as the great patriarch, the man of superb wisdom, the leader trained in the Roman tradition, who weighed carefully every question and only after mature consideration took action, the one who saw the two sides to every problem and carefully stepped between them with the grace that discretion and prudence gave him. Serene and un-rattled, unruffled and unperturbed, the man is an embodiment of everything we mean when we speak of the man of wisdom, the wise old man, the *senex*. That is why the stone statue of Saint Benedict I love so much was set up in the back woods over the wall where hardly anyone would see it. It does not reflect our idea of Benedict; much too youthful, much too disturbing, indeed much too funny. No one could take it seriously, not in terms of the image we have of the Saint.

Fancy Saint Benedict doing anything as childish as dipping a plane to greet a monk, even if we do cross the centuries to make him pilot of a Cessna. Fancy him doing something so irresponsible as ignoring sound advice about someone coming to work for him. Benedict would not do that sort of thing. I would correct that and say that the kind of Benedict we admire would not. But I am not so sure that the Benedict we admire has much to do with reality. The image is too one-sided. *Senex* must always be balanced with *puer*, you know that. The wise old man has his counterpart and the counterpart is so much a part of the whole that to admit it is to end with distortion. The *Puer Aeternus*, the eternal youth, must go with the *Senex*, the Wise Old Man. This is the archetypal understanding.

Youth is innovative and original, inventive and inspired. Youth is ingenious for a fresh approach, for taking a chance and daring to do the bold and the new. Youth is intuitive and penetrates to the heart of a question with sure instinct. Youth is willing to risk and begin anew, tired of the old and weary, of the hackneyed. Without a youthful side you turn Benedict into a dreary old man, safe and sure, an old gentleman sitting in an old English club passing out sage comment on current scene, most of it negative. Such a saint would certainly have no appeal to young men.

I think John XXIII is much closer to the real Saint Benedict. Old in years, to be sure, so old they thought him safe enough until things settled down for a real pope. But his youthful spirit rose to the occasion and he shook weary cardinals who had not had a new idea since their twenties and threw consternation into tired minds by suggesting a Council. The nerve of the man!

We monks are sometimes like tired old cardinals. We will accept anything except being disturbed, go along with anything except a new idea, tolerate any suffering except having our routine upset, our ideas changed. Sometimes I am reminded of an old lady going about with a check in her hand, going to one bank after another to get it cashed, a check twenty years old on a bank that no longer exists for money that long since disappeared. It is like a priest still clutching his biretta and complaining that no one uses the word purgatory any more. Living in yesterday and having some notion that this is wisdom, we reckon is championing the tried and the true. Say rather, the tired and the tedious.

It takes both the male and the female aspects of the human being to make a real person, my dear friends. The all-male man is a very sick one. So, too, the ideal of the old man as the epitome of wisdom is to misunderstand history, for unless youth goes along with age, then old age is a disease and not an achievement.

You need read only the first word of the rule of Saint Benedict and you get the message. You know the word: *Ausculta*, listen! Listening is not the prerogative of the old man. Just the opposite; you listen to him. He has long since given up listening. And yet we must listen, to the woods, to the sound of rain, to the history that evolves around us, to others and what they are saying, what they are doing and thinking. Most of all, we must listen to our own heart and to the Spirit active there. The point of silence is in the listening. We have lots of silence and little listening. Such a silence is too noisy.

One could describe, in detail, what characterizes the old man, the *senex*, and what characterizes the youth, the eternal young; and best of all the combination of both in some great figure. Still, if you want a test as to whether someone is on the right road, I think there is one: humor. Anyone who takes self too seriously certainly has no youthful spirit. Someone who cannot laugh at self lacks the honesty essential to real wisdom. In my image of Benedict, he is just about to laugh, the smile already on the lips, the eyes ready. The grim do not get the point. They miss the joke. Such people are generally irritable, always seem about to explode, and live on the edge of exasperation.

We cannot forget that none of this is a matter of exploit, of achievement. This is not something we set out to do, some goal we set our heart on, something we bend our will to and so make come about. Ah, no. It is much easier than that. It is simply a matter of option, of choice, of willingness, a matter of exposure. It is like having sense enough *not* to come in out of the rain, brains enough to respond to an inspiration, courage enough to listen, nerve enough to be like Christ and give it all away. It is like letting the dead bury their dead and walking on water because he suggested it, forgetting everything and setting out after him because he requested it. God be praised, we have not made a wise old man out of Christ the Lord. He died so young. Yet he is a patriarch, Wisdom itself. He is the serenity of the everlasting hills and the peace that comes of reconciling all things in himself. How youthful! How daring! How wild were his statements, his claims! It is only because we are used to them that we are unaware of how exciting is the Lord Jesus.

That is the sort of man Saint Benedict was, and that is why thousands and thousands have followed after him, just as they did Francis and Ignatius and how many others who combined in their characters that marvelous combination of the wisdom of years and the glow of youth which is so Christ-like.

29

Lost in a Rain Forest ♣

I met a bishop from Bolivia last week, and he told me of a young missionary who learned early the hazards of the rain forest, woods so dark and deep that even at mid-day one can easily be lost forever. He left the river, the usual highway, and started on foot to a far village along a path marked by gashes in trees at intervals. He managed well enough, until, lost in his thoughts, he discovered that he had lost his path and, soon afterwards, that he could not find it again. Mind you, he had only gone a few hundred yards, as far as the traffic light out in front of our monastery. And then he began to panic, realizing too late that he should never have violated the jungle's first law: never travel alone. He wandered in the rain forest three days before he found the river and safety. He never did find that path again.

This is how he managed it. He got himself calmed down and worked out a strategy. He marked the big tree right beside him with an axe on all sides, and then slowly began to make paths out from that tree in every direction, marking every step clearly. He would venture out a way, return, then move around the circle a bit, repeat the process, and slowly worked his way round the tree and out from it, going further from that center each time. Eventually he came to the river. He was three days doing it. His tactic was a good one and saved his life. I suggest that it is a good one for us too.

We all need a center to which to return. We all need a base, a point to which and from which. We all need some *locus* to which we should be related. We all need some sort of hope, some harbor, some retreat.

Today in the gospel we heard the heart of the gospel message, the Beatitudes, so called from the first word of each portion: *beati*, blessed are they . . . , happy are they . . . . There is no more dynamic, no more dramatic and beautiful expression of our faith than that given us by Jesus in the Sermon on the Mount. And, of course, for it must be said, none more impractical. Could you base a life on the Beatitudes? Maybe that is not what they are for in the first place. But it is good to return to them often to get some sort of focus in our vision, some clarity of outlook, some finding of our way in the dark of this life and our pointless wandering around in it.

We need to hear that money is not everything, not even money held in common. Neither are place and position and power and influence and reputation and competence and accomplishment and achievement and being somebody and amounting to something, making a strong assertion and making that self-assertion stick. The Beatitudes tell us that this is not it, this is not what we are here for. Here is not happiness. There is more to life than grubbing, even grubbing for what is eminently worth grubbing for.

That is why the Beatitudes are impractical. Does anyone take them seriously? Save as poetry? Or are they for those who do not make it—the poor, for example, the bankrupt, the failures, the ne'er-do-wells, the ones put to death or sentenced to jail, the miserably sick, the victims of society's triumphs, the debris of war, maybe, the fruit of our economics, the people who make profit possible; in short, the multitudes on earth whose life is not as good as that of a wandering dog. These he calls blessed.

Our return to the center is not a return to some code of behavior, some set of ethical practices, a few words to live by. Christianity is not a book, or a code, a set of precepts, but a Person. We do not travel the dark woods of this life alone: we go with Christ. Even with him we are often lost and confused, misled, mistaken, so weak is our faith. But without him, we simply wander round in a circle, just like so many who never get anywhere.

If you would taste a little happiness, then listen to the One who told us where to find it. Since he made the deep woods and knows the darkness of the human heart, it is likely he can find his way in them and help us do the same. The choice is ours, not his. That marked tree is still there deep in the jungle of northern Bolivia. The sign of Christ's wounded body is meaningless and useless with no one to make it a center. The gospel is nothing without us. With us it is a Word of life, the way through, the way out, the way in. Amen.

30

THE SIGN OF JONAH ❧

'**A**n evil and adulterous generation seeks for a sign, but
no sign shall be given it, except the sign of the prophet
Jonah.' (Mt 12:39) Jonah, in this wonderful story, did
not obey God. In many ways he was a poor prophet, and yet
he is the sign, the only sign, given to this evil and adulterous
generation. Bidden to go to Nineveh, Jonah went instead to a
distant land in the opposite direction—and he knew what he
was doing. Jonah was in flight from the Lord. Yet Jonah was, as
we know, the concern of a strange providence.

Who was this Jonah? Is this story fact or fiction, when did it
happen, did it happen— these things are irrelevant. The book
of Jonah is the word of God and has a message. This message,
this point, is what interests us. What is the point? And first of
all, who is Jonah?

Jonah, first of all, is Jesus, Jesus running away from God,
leaving heaven behind him, not, indeed, in a precise sense, but
in that he identified himself with humankind, with man running
from God. Jonah is Jesus because it is Jesus who acknowledges
guilt and takes on blame, takes upon himself the guilt of humanity, the sin of the world. Jonah is Jesus because it is Jesus
who wills to be cast into the deep by his own, sacrificed in
order to placate the Lord God, put to death as the guilty one
responsible for the plight we are in. Jonah is Jesus because the
Father delivers him from the realms of death after he has been
hidden three days and nights in the heart of the earth. It is the
Father who raises Jesus from the dead, who provides for his
deliverance from the deep.

Who is Jonah? I am Jonah, because I flee from the face of God, from duty and obligation and the call of grace. I turn my back on what I ought to do, on what I ought to be. I am like Jonah because, like him, I know my fault and failing. I own that I am sin and sinner, evil and adulterous. I am Jonah because, guilty like him, I am willing to be cast whole into the depths of the sea by others, deservedly put to death, only to have the waters become a saving baptism that gives new life. I am Jonah because, like him, I am swallowed by the mysterious fish that hides me in its bosom for three days and nights and then brings me up on the shores of a new world in God.

After he was left on the beach by the great fish that had borne him, Jonah did his duty. He went on to Nineveh and preached repentance to the people of that mighty city. He told them that after forty days, unless they were converted from their ways, the city would be laid waste. So the inhabitants, mighty and lowly, human and beast too, began a fast. They did penance. The Ninevites converted in their hearts and the Lord repented and spared them.

And now Jonah, a many-sided man, revealed a new aspect. He was envious of the good fortune that had come to Nineveh and was angry that God should be so good to them. He complained that the Lord was not strict enough, that God was too prone to mercy and forbearance. Jonah pouted and took himself outside the city to nurse his hurt feelings in solitude. God raised up a castor bean plant to give shade from the heat of the sun and Jonah was touched by the kindness. But his good mood soon turned to complaining when a worm gnawed the vine and it collapsed around him. He insisted angrily that God might have spared him the plant, small thing that it was. God then chided him for his pettiness, that he would make a fuss over a castor bean plant and think nothing at all of condemning a whole city—men, women, children, cattle and all.

Why did Jonah run from God in the first place and stiffen his heart against the Lord? And why did Jonah begrudge the good that God did for others through him? And why did

Jonah complain of the trifling trial God sent him in having the worm bring down the shady vine? Because Jonah, though aware indeed of his own sins and failings, was not aware of the great love that God bore him. He did not see the first call as an act of God's love, not just a demand made on him. He did not see his act of sacrifice for the men on the ship as pleasing to God—not just the decent thing to do, but the only thing he could do. He did not see the three days and nights in the belly of the fish as God's love at work—not just good luck, a lucky break. He did not see that he was a vessel of grace for the Ninevites—not just a man doing his job. He did not appreciate the fact that love was behind all that God did, that God has great love for every person alive, for every living thing.

So, who is Jonah? You are Jonah when your heart is dull to goodness, when you do not respond to the call of beauty. You are Jonah when, like him, you are unwilling to admit that God can work good through you, when you do not believe that, in spite of your failings, the grace of God is with you, that there is beauty within you. You are Jonah when, like him, you envy the good God does for others, as Jonah was envious of the Ninevites. Not seeing his own beauty, he could not tolerate beauty in others. You are Jonah when, like him, you complain of small sufferings. He was angry with God for taking away the shady vine; we are angry with God for trivial trials, but when our feeling for beauty is small, God will always encourage its growth by sending suffering. The original Jonah, in spite of himself, was an instrument of good. He was at the same time an object of God's tender care and a sign for all the world of the power of Jesus' love. If, like Jonah, you are imperfect, then rejoice that even so, God may be manifested in you by divine mercy, and will be made more manifest by making your dullness of heart turn to openness of spirit, your envy to joy over good, your anger to thoughts of peace, your resentment to acceptance of love, acknowledgement of beauty.

Jonah is every person in flight from God, aware of guilt, plunging into the maternal waters from which life sprang, being reborn after this passion and death, discovering God's great love for all creation. Jesus, the hidden Jonah, risen from the dead after three days in the tomb, will come at the end of time, at the fulfillment of all things, to judge whether we were willing to be a Jonah, to be a sign; willing to accept our need for repentance and compunction, and to act on that need by casting ourselves totally into the sea of God's mercy—the act that moves the hearts of others aboard the ship, the act that converts the Ninevites of our day—so that we may share in the salvation of our evil and adulterous generation.

The sign of Jonah is the sign given this generation, then, because it is a sign of love. It tells us that the life and death of Our Lord, the three days and three nights in the heart of the earth, the glorious rising, is a work of love. It is our own birth, and death, and descent into the waters of primordial chaos, our own rising to live in beauty, and is already begun, already being accomplished. The people of Nineveh will judge us on the last day if we do not reckon with the sign of Jonah, if we do not understand the beauty of love and its secret presence everywhere, do not realize that to believe in love is the greatest thing we can do. The beauty of Jesus' love about us, within us, all around us is a radiance in the heart of everything that is, in my own heart most of all.

'An evil and adulterous generation seeks a sign and no sign shall be given it except the sign of the prophet Jonah.'

31

ONE WITH THE WORLD ❧

'You have learnt how it was said: Eye for eye and tooth for tooth. *But I say this to you: offer the wicked man no resistance. On the contrary, if anyone hits you on the right cheek, offer him the other as well; if a man takes you to law and would have your tunic, let him have your cloak as well. And if anyone orders you to go one mile, go two miles with him. Give to anyone who asks, and if anyone wants to borrow, do not turn away. You have learnt how it was said:* You must love your neighbor *and hate your enemy. But I say this to you: love your enemies and pray for those who persecute you; in this way you will be sons of your Father in heaven, for he causes his sun to rise on bad men as well as good, and his rain to fall on honest and dishonest men alike. For if you love those who love you, what right have you to claim any credit? Even the tax collectors do as much, do they not? And if you save your greetings for your brothers, are you doing anything exceptional? Even the pagans do as much, do they not? You must therefore be perfect just as your heavenly Father is perfect.* (Matthew 5:38–48)

After the reading of the gospel passage this morning, one can only think how they must have loved that man! The boldness of it. The nerve of it. 'You have heard how it was said . . . but I say to you.'

They resented him too, were angry at him. No one likes being unsettled, really. No one likes having solid positions challenged, assured verities questioned. Not you and I. We are famous for loving peace, that is, for being left alone, for not being upset, not having our monastic tranquillity disturbed. I think the gospel reminds us this morning that if we are not now and then shaken to our roots by the word of the Lord and his action on us, among us, in us, then (it can be assumed) we are out of touch, no longer with it, no longer among the living. So, the first question is, how long since you have been rattled by the Lord? Or, in the words of an ad I read at Christmas time, how long since you had your socks knocked off?

Twenty-five years ago this winter I came to this monastery for the first time. It seems only yesterday. I was a middle-aged priest then and at odds with things, as one often is at that period of life. I fell in love with the place at once. A number of things were involved, but there was one in particular. And that one thing was this: this was the first group of celibate men I had known who were able to be tender and gentle, who were not afraid to be as they liked.

They are more gentle today than they were then and still not afraid to be as they like, able to take their cue from a spirit that is not that of the world around them. I was completely at a loss to account for it. As individuals the monks were not and are not all that exceptional. The place, as such, has not that much going for it, then or now. One ecclesiastic of position at his first look said it was the ugliest religious house he knew. A travelled European he. I later came to the conclusion that it was the wall, that symbolic structure that tells the rest of the world that inside is ours and we do as we like, when we like, if we like.

In other words, this was the first place I had ever been where I could be free. It is a house of freedom, freedom from the awful tyranny the world imposes. And what tyranny most of all? That macho culture which imposes aggression and competition and assertion and strife and contention and says that this is the way to live, this is natural, normal, human, and, above all, 'manly'.

I have news for you. It is nothing of the sort. It is a diseased form of living. A sick society lives by such ideals. It is as weird and queer a kind of living as the world has ever known. Everything—even song and dance and drama and the cult of the noblest gifts—is permeated by this way. Ask anyone in law school, in art school, in medical school, in music school, what it is like. They will tell you what it is like: a vicious jungle.

This is spirit which breeds war, cultivates it and blesses it, nobles and sanctifies it. Humanity dedicates to that horror the totality of its gifts, its resources, the brilliance of its best minds, the talents of its most lavishly endowed. Science is in the service of war. War is the biggest business we have, we, the biggest country in the world. And business is good. I do not think it possible to be a Christian and be committed to such a world.

So, I came here to a world within a world, where ordinary men can become ordinary Christians and not have to apologize for it. We believe in love and in patience and in tolerance and in forbearance. We believe in littleness and forgiveness. This is not a house of self-assertion and self-aggrandizement. We do not cultivate contention, or reward pushy go-getters. We praise service and humility, gentleness and dedication, the love of beauty, pretty clothes and pretty music and pretty ceremony, song and dance in the night, bells ringing for joy, for sorrow, incense making the air blue with fragrance and flowers cluttering up our ways. This is a house of counter-revolution, a center of rebellion. This nay-saying stronghold knows another way, sings another song: it not only listens to a different drum, but beats it for all who can hear, a world away from that hideous scene called the pursuit of excellence.

But we are still much in the world, one with it, but one with the world of the troubled and trodden upon, those untold millions who make up the poor suckers of the capitalist kingdom, those currently rejected from the working scene, those left by the way as incompetent: the inept, the unable, the old, the stupid, and above all the poor, the poor who don't make it.

In his book *Origins*, Richard Leakey says that early man's characteristic, was cooperation and not for centuries, not for millenia, but literally for millions of years. This is by far the basic relation of human to human: cooperation. Competition and strife are something new. The old saw that puts aggression in our genes, as something native to us, is a gross blunder and a neat convenience. The teaching of Jesus, then, far from being something out of this world and impractical and mythical, is something within our reach. It is as natural to us as the supernatural.

The news then, my dear friends, is not that you are special, but that you are common, normal: not the freakish but the ordinary. In following Jesus and his way, we are not only close to God but close to our true humanity. To be like Jesus: that is the ideal. To be as tough, as gentle, as rooted in love.

The other day I went over to Nazareth convent to buy some books for a New Guinea nun. I visited the graves of the sisters there, 1,488 graves. Think of that. What a sight, what a moving sight! Whole fields sown with love. What a vision. Women have served Jesus so well and in such numbers.

It is the oddest thing, is it not? The teaching of Jesus that in the world sounds so far out, so wild, so extravagant, is really not that at all. It is the worldly world around us that is far out, that is weird and crazy. In New Guinea, making Christians of the people was nothing at all. The Good News was good news to them. They took to it and loved it. But making capitalists of them? That was something else. Too alien in spirit. So the foreigners wake up and realize that the Christian veneer over cheap capitalism is deception and fraud. Nothing betrays religion like religion.

'You heard it said', the Lord is saying, 'you heard it said. But I say to you'. Say on, good Lord.

32

MEDITATIONS ON THE EUCHARIST ♣

I.

Ancient cities had narrow gates. This was the only possible way to defend them. Toll gates on our throughways are very narrow. There is no other way to collect the toll from each vehicle. It is in the nature of things that there will be difficulties. How much of our complaint and grumbling is basically unrealistic. Christ tells us to be realistic, to have common sense, in looking at things.

II.

A blue block at your place used to mean that you wanted no soup. Father Louis told us novices that we didn't rate a blue block, only the professed did. We were to live the common life and eat the common soup, to take our chances. The blue-blood people of the Boston that I came from had one hard-and-fast rule about life: their names and their faces never appeared in public places. The common life was not for them. In a spirit of repentance we might ask ourselves if we dare the common life, can risk the soup.

III.

The new bishop of Boston said that after Boston there is only heaven. Those of you who know Boston will not find this hard to accept. Even more true, I suspect, is to say that after Gethsemani there is only heaven. Indeed, that is true of any place. May we live in the hope of heaven and thus find joy where we live on earth.

IV.

There is no social body on earth that so neatly combines the old and the new, tradition and innovation, as the Catholic Church, if for no other reason that it is the oldest organization of humankind. Doctrinal development is always both innovative and traditional and so in some way unites the conservative and the liberal. It is easy to be one thing or the other. What is very arduous, in this as in so much else of life, is to combine both. One-sidedness is a kind of sin, a false emphasis and a distortion. We might think about that.

V.

Maybe you have noticed the two kinds of workers we have in the assembly line over at Fun City—where the cheese is packed—these days. There are monks who stop working while they talk, and monks who can talk and keep right on working. There are extroverts and introverts, those who take the exterior world seriously and give their full attention to one thing at a time and people to whom the only real world and the only one to take seriously is the inner. Two sorts of people living in two different worlds. It is not good to be a Peter and to decide by yourself what is good for Alexis. It is better to be like Jesus and let even a blind man speak for himself and not organize his life for him. The introvert does not live in the extrovert's world and I certainly do not live in yours.

VI.

He and I were coming over the New Haven road in a little Toyota very early in the morning. It was still dark. We came over the brow of the hill and I said, 'There is the abbey, all lit up. They are in church.' 'I know,' he said. 'I am familiar with it.' But he did not slow down and he did not turn in. And I said, 'But aren't you coming in?' in a hurt tone. 'No,' he said. 'I came to call sinners, not the righteous.' 'But we are sinners,' I said, 'not righteous.' 'Well, if that is the way it is, all right.' And at the old mill gate he turned back. And we came in. Everyone was ready for Mass and I was standing here and I said,

Lord, we have sinned against you.
Lord, show us your mercy and your love.
May Almighty God have mercy on us, forgive us our sins,
   and bring us to everlasting life.

VII.

The monk comes to the tailor shop for pants. He is a 38 and we have 36 and we have 40, but no 38. He is annoyed and wonders why he cannot get an answer to his quest. It happens often. We have a choice, but it is not a real choice. We feel had. It is like Christ coming, usually at the wrong time and thus never expected. Tires go flat, shoestrings break, typewriter ribbons run out—always at the wrong time. These odd things happen because so much of our life is odd and not synchronized with God's will. I hazard that hunch as we enter into this mystery. God Almighty, we are often exasperated at your coming to us in the inept and inadequate events that characterize our lives. Be thou gracious and bring good out of awkward moments, success out of hard choices, and peace from our frequent fury. Through Christ our Lord.

VIII.

A man called from California and asked for a Mass to be said. Nothing new, but, his case being urgent, he wanted the Mass offered by 'a very holy priest'. That is something else, I thought; not *who* is the holy priest, but *what* is a holy priest? So I ask you, what is a holy monk? A worker of miracles today, a very pious man, a man of penance, a warm tolerant charitable man, a learned man whose learning is put to the service of the community, a hard worker, a dutiful member? Think on that if you will and on what your idea of holiness is. Put it in two or three words, your ideal. And let me ask you, how are you doing?

IX.

Not long ago a woman from a far away place wrote in, asking for some Masses to be said for her ancestors on her side and on her husband's side. She felt there had been a murder in the line somewhere that needed to be atoned for, because ill fortune had overcome a beloved son who was deep into drugs. Is this thinking bizarre? Do we carry inherited evil? I turn the question to you and merely note that we are involved with one another in profound ways, living and dead, we humans. Our sorrow for sin before we approach this altar today is at once singular and communal, for us, for all.

X.

When the Virgin sat by the shore, watching the fishermen with the child asleep in her arms, she thought long thoughts; that web, that net of what was, what is, and what is to be. We insert into that mystery the voice of prayer for ourselves, for others, for those who are, who were, and who will be.

XI.

Self-assertion builds competition, and competition is the life of trade, and trade is what capitalism is all about. Self-denial builds community, and community is life in love, and love is what Christianity is all about. Let us in prayer ask God to take from us and give to those in need.

XII.

A man named Iococca heard from another man named Lombardi something I believe Saint Paul would have enjoyed. It was that a good team requires competent people who are well-disciplined. But this is not enough to make winners. To be winners they have to love one another. Not bad, coming from a world of automobiles and football. Disciplined competence alone can make a *prima donna* who uses the team to show off plumage and not her plumage to show off the team. Love, like bourbon in a fruit cake, makes all the difference in the world.

XIII.

I suppose you've noticed that it is rather difficult in the human comedy to do any good without at the same time doing evil. You innocently decide to mow some grass to tidy a roadside and you end up destroying young trees your brother had carefully planted in another season. Christ is born in Bethlehem and a host of youngsters his age are put to death because of it. Peter is rescued from prison by an angel and Herod executes the guards set to watch him. In this strange world of darkness and light we need to live in mercy, mercy earnestly asked for, happily received, and generously given. If we do evil when we set out to do good, what happens when we are not at our best?

XIV.

There is surely no religion as utterly earthy as our own. It is taken up with conception and pregnancy and birth, not to say life itself, together with suffering and death. It is a religion that says with equal insistence that all these times and all these events are filled with God. We must feel a bit like Pope John XXIII who, putting his arms around a blind boy, said to him, 'I will pray for you. You pray for me, for I am blind too.'

XV.

My older brother led a rather wild and tumultuous life and in the end took to wandering around the country, a free and independent spirit, now in touch, now not. He lay dying in a federal hospital at Boston harbor when, one Sunday afternoon, a young man from the Vincent de Paul Society came by to do the patients small favors and wrote a letter for my brother to me—about the only name and address he could remember. I got word to his sons and daughters and so he died with a priest and with his family around him and had a nice funeral in the old parish church. This is what Saint Vincent de Paul is all about, I think: small favors to small people. In our good concern for global issues, let us not forget small favors and little kindnesses.

XVI.

Our vocational literature notes that candidates will not find the world of the computer here at the abbey. That was written fifteen years ago. It is no longer true. But there is a truth in it. We are not apt to be first with the latest. We move rather slowly. Sometimes very slowly. We got electric lights in the choir in the late 1920s, I think. There is a quality in our life that we cherish but that can easily be lost. It is precious, delicate, subtle. So we take our time. We can ask Saint Joseph to help us be people he would recognize as his kind. And we repent of dissimilarity, even in our work life, maybe most of all in our work life.

XVII.

A former novice told me he was very troubled one time. A monk saw him in choir, saw that he was distressed, sought him privately and took him in his arms, comforted him, laid his head against his breast. The man told me, years later, 'You know, I could hear his heart beat, the first time I ever heard a human heart.' And I said, 'Oh, no. A long time ago, in the shadows of your past, in the infinite mystery of your beginnings in the delightful darkness of your mother's womb, you heard her heart And it was the sound of a loving heart that you missed so, needed so. And once you heard that sound all the primordial memories came back and brought you comfort.'

I do not think that troubled people are rare. We all at sometime know anxiety and fears. Nor do I doubt the presence of many loving hearts. Yet I daresay there are times when we, too, need to hear the sound of a loving heart, for it is a testimony of the great loving heart of God that beats for us for ever.

XVIII.

Flannery O'Conner bequeathed her peacocks to Holy Spirit monastery in Georgia where they continued for a long time to display the daring of God Almighty, who could combine in one creature the dazzling beauty of the peacock's plumage and the shrieking screech of its voice. That is a good reminder of the human situation. We are at once far more beautiful than any peacock, yet in some ways more hideous. Hence our cry for mercy.

XIX.

We are sympathetic with those who know pain which we have known, but find it hard to be moved by what is remote from us. A fruitful use of suffering is enriching. The communion of saints is a sharing in the passion. Our prayer reflects this. God Almighty, make our compassion genuine through our willingness to know you in every season, to be with you in all kinds of weather, to be true to you. Through Christ our Lord.

XX.

We speak of places and persons as haunted when they are frequented by the presence of the past. We are all haunted by those we have known and loved when times gone come back to us and are relived. This earth is haunted by the memory of Christ, an enduring presence more real than we can possibly imagine, since it is his very spirit which abides with us in him. We think then how we have failed in not softening sorrow over loss with the sense of presence that surrounds us always.

XXI.

We commemorate today [April 29] not merely a number of holy abbots of Cluny, but perhaps better a whole historic movement rising out of one center, one of the most glorious in the whole of Europe's history. We need to recall, though, that movements and orders and houses are people, and that we are judged individually, whether we live in a house or an order or a time of glory and splendor or something less. History is not within our control. What sort of people we are is.

XXII.

The novitiate used to be out back, with Father Louis. The gift shop was out front, with Brother Ralph. One day Father Louis had a visitor, a Jewish friend from New York, whom he met out front and brought in through the gift shop, making a sweeping gesture as he passed saying 'This is the pious junk which simple people buy when they come here'. Brother Ralph overheard the remark and, vexed, sat down and wrote a note, not trusting himself to the customary signs of those days. 'Dear Father Louis,' he wrote. 'I did not appreciate your remark to your friend this morning. You know as well as I do that the pious junk in this shop was here before I took over and I am doing all I can to get rid of it. Meanwhile, I am doing the best I can to build up a good inventory. If you think you can do any better, you are welcome to come and do so. Love, Brother Ralph.'

A day or so later I went to see Father Louis, knowing nothing of this.

'Benedicte!'

'Sit down a minute; I am just finishing a note to Brother Ralph. Be right with you'.

By way of conversation I said, 'And what would you be writing Brother Ralph about?' 'Here,' he said, 'Read his note.' I read it as he finished and asked him, 'And what did you tell the Brother?' 'Why, I apologized, of course. I had no business making such a remark.' Nice story.

We all offend with the tongue, some of us more than others. It is good to apologize for it, both to God and to our brother, good to have pity on the poor we live with who must suffer from what we inflict on them.

> From a sharp and biting tongue,
> keep us, O Lord.
> Lord have mercy!

From sarcastic remarks and smart-aleck words,
keep us O Lord.
   Christ, have mercy!

From angry retorts and snippy responses,
keep us, O Lord.
   Lord, have mercy!

CISTERCIAN PUBLICATIONS, INC.
TITLES LISTING

—CISTERCIAN TEXTS—

THE WORKS OF
BERNARD OF CLAIRVAUX

Apologia to Abbot William
Five Books on Consideration: Advice to a Pope
Homilies in Praise of the Blessed Virgin Mary
The Life and Death of Saint Malachy the Irishman
Love without Measure. Extracts from the Writings
  of St Bernard (Paul Dimier)
On Grace and Free Choice
On Loving God (Emero Stiegman)
The Parables of Saint Bernard (Michael Casey)
Sermons for the Summer Season
Sermons on Conversion
Sermons on the Song of Songs I - IV
The Steps of Humility and Pride

THE WORKS OF
WILLIAM OF SAINT THIERRY

The Enigma of Faith
Exposition on the Epistle to the Romans
Exposition on the Song of Songs
The Golden Epistle
The Mirror of Faith
The Nature of Dignity of Love
On Contemplating God, Prayer & Meditations

THE WORKS OF AELRED OF RIEVAULX

Dialogue on the Soul
Liturgical Sermons, I
The Mirror of Charity
Spiritual Friendship
Treatises I: On Jesus at the Age of Twelve, Rule for a
  Recluse, The Pastoral Prayer
Walter Daniel: The Life of Aelred of Rievaulx

THE WORKS OF JOHN OF FORD

Sermons on the Final Verses of the Songs of Songs
  I - VII

THE WORKS OF GILBERT OF HOYLAND

Sermons on the Songs of Songs I-III
Treatises, Sermons and Epistles

OTHER EARLY CISTERCIAN WRITERS

The Letters of Adam of Perseigne I
Alan of Lille: The Art of Preaching
Baldwin of Ford: Spiritual Tractates I - II
Gertrud the Great of Helfta: Spiritual Exercises
Gertrud the Great of Helfta: The Herald of God's
  Loving-Kindness
Guerric of Igny: Liturgical Sermons I -[II]
Idung of Prüfening: Cistercians and Cluniacs: The
  Case of Cîteaux
Isaac of Stella: Sermons on the Christian Year,I - [II]
The Life of Beatrice of Nazareth
Serlo of Wilton & Serlo of Savigny: Works
Stephen of Lexington: Letters from Ireland
Stephen of Sawley: Treatises

—MONASTIC TEXTS—

EASTERN CHRISTIAN TRADITION

Besa: The Life of Shenoute
Cyril of Scythopolis: Lives of the Monks of Palestine
Dorotheos of Gaza: Discourses and Sayings
Evagrius Ponticus:Praktikos and Chapters on Prayer
Handmaids of the Lord: The Lives of Holy Women in
  Late Antiquity & the Early Middle Ages
  (Joan Petersen)
The Harlots of the Desert (Benedicta Ward)
John Moschos: The Spiritual Meadow
The Lives of the Desert Fathers
The Lives of Simeon Stylites (Robert Doran)
The Luminous Eye (Sebastian Brock)
Mena of Nikiou: Isaac of Alexandra & St Macrobius
Pachomian Koinonia I - III (Armand Veilleux)
Paphnutius: A Histories of the Monks of Upper Egypt
The Sayings of the Desert Fathers (B. Ward)
Spiritual Direction in the Early Christian East (Irénée
  Hausherr)
Spiritually Beneficial Tales of Paul, Bishop of
  Monembasia (John Wortley)
Symeon the New Theologian: The Theological and
  Practical Treatises & The Three Theological
  Discourses (P. McGuckin)
Theodoret of Cyrrhus: A History of the Monks of Syria
The Syriac Fathers on Prayer and the Spiritual Life
  (Sebastian Brock)

WESTERN CHRISTIAN TRADITION

Anselm of Canterbury: Letters I - III (W. Fröhlich)
Bede: Commentary on the Acts of the Apostles
Bede: Commentary on the Seven Catholic Epistles
Bede: Homilies on the Gospels I - II
The Celtic Monk (U. O Maidin)
Gregory the Great: Forty Gospel Homilies
The Meditations of Guigo I, Prior of the Charterhouse
  (A. Gordon Mursell)
Peter of Celle: Selected Works
The Letters of Armand-Jean de Rancé I - II
The Rule of the Master
The Rule of Saint Augustine
The Wound of Love: A Carthusian Miscellany

CHRISTIAN SPIRITUALITY

Abba: Guides to Wholeness & Holiness East & West
A Cloud of Witnesses: The Development of Christian
  Doctrine (D.N. Bell)
The Call of Wild Geese (M. Kelty)
Cistercian Way (André Louf)
The Contemplative Path
Drinking From the Hidden Fountain (T. Spidlík)
Eros and Allegory: Medieval Exegesis of the Song of
  Songs (Denys Turner)
Fathers Talking (Aelred Squire)
Friendship and Community (B. McGuire)
From Cloister to Classroom
The Silent Herald of Unity: The Life of Maria Gabrielle
  Sagheddu (M. Driscoll)
Life of St Mary Magdalene and of Her Sister
  St Martha (D. Mycoff)

Many Mansions (D. N. Bell)
The Name of Jesus (Irénée Hausherr)
No Moment Too Small (Norvene Vest)
Penthos: The Doctrine of Compunction in the
    Christian East (Irénée Hausherr)
Rancé and the Trappist Legacy (A.J. Krailsheimer)
The Roots of the Modern Christian Tradition
Russian Mystics (S. Bolshakoff)
Sermons in A Monastery (M. Kelty)
The Spirituality of the Christian East (Tomas Spidlík)
The Spirituality of the Medieval West (André Vauchez)
Tuning In To Grace (André Louf)
Wholly Animals: A Book of Beastly Tales (D.N. Bell)

—MONASTIC STUDIES—

Community & Abbot in the Rule of St Benedict I - II
    (Adalbert De Vogüé)
The Finances of the Cistercian Order in the
    Fourteenth Century (Peter King)
Fountains Abbey & Its Benefactors (Joan Wardrop)
The Hermit Monks of Grandmont (Carole A.
    Hutchison)
In the Unity of the Holy Spirit (Sighard Kleiner)
The Joy of Learning & the Love of God: Essays in
    Honor of Jean Leclercq
Monastic Practices (Charles Cummings)
The Occupation of Celtic Sites in Ireland by the
    Canons Regular of St Augustine and the
    Cistercians (Geraldine Carville)
Reading Saint Benedict (Adalbert de Vogüé)
The Rule of St Benedict: A Doctrinal and Spiritual
    Commentary (Adalbert de Vogüé)
The Rule of St Benedict (Br. Pinocchio)
Serving God First (Sighard Kleiner)
St Hugh of Lincoln (D.H. Farmer)
Stones Laid Before the Lord (A. Dimier)
What Nuns Read (D. N. Bell)
With Greater Liberty: A Short History of Christian
    Monasticism & Religious Orders (K. Frank)

—CISTERCIAN STUDIES—

Aelred of Rievaulx: A Study (A. Squire)
Athirst for God: Spiritual Desire in Bernard of
    Clairvaux's Sermonson the the Song of Songs
    (M. Casey)
Beatrice of Nazareth in Her Context
    (Roger De Ganck)
Bernard of Clairvaux & the Cistercian Spirit
    (Jean Leclercq)
Bernard of Clairvaux: Man, Monk, Mystic
    (M. Casey) Tapes and readings
Bernard of Clairvaux: Studies Presented to Dom Jean
    Leclercq
Bernardus Magister (Nonacentenary)
Christ the Way: The Christology of Guerric of Igny
    (John Morson)
Cistercian Sign Language (R. Barakat)
The Cistercian Spirit
The Cistercians in Denmark (Brian McGuire)
The Cistercians in Scandinavia (James France)
A Difficult Saint (B. McGuire)

The Eleventh-century Background of Cîteaux
    (Bede K. Lackner)
A Gathering of Friends: Learning & Spirituality in John
    of Forde (Costello and Holdsworth)
Image and Likeness: The Augustinian Spirituality
    of William of St Thierry (D.N. Bell)
An Index of Authors & Works in Cistercian Libraries in
    Great Britain I (D.N. Bell)
The Mystical Theology of St Bernard (Etiénne Gilson)
Nicolas Cotheret's Annals of Cîteaux (Louis J. Lekai)
A Second Look at Saint Bernard (J.Leclercq)
The Spiritual Teachings of St Bernard of Clairvaux
    (J.R. Sommerfeldt)
Studiosorum Speculum [L. J. Lekai]
Towards Unification with God (Beatrice of Nazareth
    in Her Context, 2)
William, Abbot of St Thierry
Women and St Bernard of Clairvaux (Jean Leclercq)

—MEDIEVAL RELIGIOUS— WOMEN
Lillian Thomas Shank and John A. Nichols, editors

Distant Echoes
Peace Weavers
Hidden Springs: Cistercian Monastic Women, 2 Vol.

—CARTHUSIAN TRADITION—

The Call of Silent Love
Guigo II: The Ladder of Monks & Twelve Meditations
    (Colledge & Walsh)
Meditations of Guigo II (A. G. Mursell)
The Way of Silent Love (A Carthusian Miscellany)
The Wound of Love (A Carthusian Miscellany)
They Speak by Silences (A Carthusian)

—STUDIES IN CISTERCIAN— ART & ARCHITECTURE
Meredith Parsons Lillich, editor

Volumes II, III and IV are now available

—THOMAS MERTON—

The Climate of Monastic Prayer (T. Merton)
The Legacy of Thomas Merton (P. Hart)
The Message of Thomas Merton (P. Hart)
The Monastic Journey of Thomas Merton (P. Hart)
Thomas Merton Monk & Artist (V. Kramer)
Thomas Merton on St Bernard
Toward an Integrated Humanity (M. Basil
    Pennington ed.)

—CISTERCIAN LITURGICAL— DOCUMENTS SERIES
Chrysogonus Waddell, ocso, editor

Hymn Collection of the Abbey of the Paracletee
Institutiones nostrae: The Paraclete Statutes
Molesme Summer-Season Breviary (4 volumes)
Old French Ordinary & Breviary of the Abbey of the
    Paraclete: Text & Commentary (2 volumes)

The Cadouin Breviary (two volumes)
The Twelfth-century Cistercian Hymnal (2 volumes)
The Twelfth-century Cistercian Psalter
The Twelfth-century Usages of the Cistercian Lay
    brothers
Two Early *Libelli Missarum*

—STUDIA PATRISTICA XVIII—
Volumes 1, 2 and 3

❖ ❖ ❖ ❖ ❖ ❖ ❖ ❖ ❖ ❖ ❖ ❖ ❖

Editorial queries & advance book information should be directed to the Editorial Offices.

Cistercian Publications
Dept. 96TLB
Institute of Cistercian Studies
Western Michigan University Station
Kalamazoo, Michigan 49008

Tel: (616) 387-8920 ❖ Fax: (616) 387-8921

❖ ❖ ❖ ❖ ❖ ❖ ❖ ❖ ❖ ❖ ❖ ❖

*A new 96-98 complete catalogue of
texts in translation and studies on
early, medieval, and modern monasti-
cism is available now at no cost from
Cistercian Publications.*

Cistercian Publications is a non-profit corpo-
ration. Its publishing program is restricted to
monastic texts in translation and books on
the monastic tradition.

*North American customers may order these books
through booksellers or directly from the warehouse,
(address below):*

Cistercian Publications (Distributor)
St Joseph's Abbey
Spencer, Massachusetts 01562

Tel: (508) 885-8730 ❖ Fax: (508) 885-4687